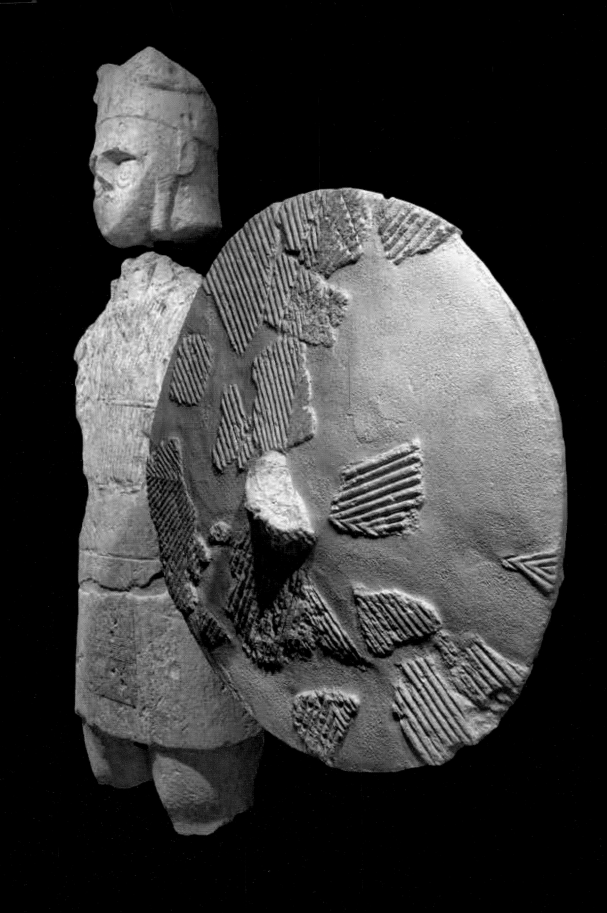

A LOST MEDITERRANEAN CULTURE

*The Giant Statues of
Sardinia's Mont'e Prama*

EDITED BY

Barbara Faedda and Paolo Carta

Columbia University Press
New York

Columbia University Press
Publishers Since 1893
New York   Chichester, West Sussex
cup.columbia.edu

Library of Congress Cataloging-in-Publication Data
Names: Faedda, Barbara, editor, writer of preface. | Carta, Paolo, editor,
    writer of preface.
Title: A lost Mediterranean culture : the giant statues of Sardinia's
    Mont'e Prama / edited by Barbara Faedda and Paolo Carta.
Description: New York : Columbia University Press, 2023. | Includes
    bibliographical references.
Identifiers: LCCN 2022062325 | ISBN 9780231212106 (hardback) |
    ISBN 9780231559218 (ebook)
Subjects: LCSH: Monte Prama Site (Italy) | Statues—Italy—Sardinia. |
    Excavations (Archaeology)—Italy—Sardinia. | Sardinia
    (Italy)—Antiquities. | Antiquities, Prehistoric—Italy—Sardinia.
Classification: LCC DG70.M6395 L67 2023 | DDC 937/.9—dc23/eng/20230111
LC record available at https://lccn.loc.gov/2022062325

Columbia University Press books are printed on permanent and durable acid-free paper.
Printed in the United States of America

Credits

Artokoloro / Alamy Stock Photo: 6.3. Basemap by Jessica Nowlin (UT San Antonio): Figure 4.1. Centro di Conservazione Archeologica—CCA Roma: 5.1-5.15. Civic Museum of San Vero Milis; with authorization from the National Archaeological Museum of Cagliari: 4.3, 4.4. © Christie's Images / Bridgeman Images: 6.2. From the excavations by A. Bedini, C. Tronchetti, and A. Usai: 1.9. Ferruccio Barreca Archaeological Museum, Sant'Antioco: 6.6. Giovanni Marongiu Civic Museum of Cabras (photo by Nicola Castangia): 1.2, 1.3 (left), 1.6, 3.1–3.3. Mont'e Prama Foundation archives: page ii. National Archaeological Museum of Cagliari (photo by Giovanni Dall'Orto): 6.4. National Archeological Museum of Cagliari (photo by Nicola Castangia): 1.1, 1.4, 1.5, 1.6, 1.8, 3.4, 3.5, 3.6, 3.7, 6.5; front cover; page vi. Photo by Giovanni Romano, VII Reparto Volo, Polizia di Stato—Oristano, sketch by Luciana Tocco: 2.2. Photo by Ivan Lucherini: 2.1. Photo by Luciana Tocco: 1.7, 2.3. Van Dommelen et al. 2020 (photo F. Pinna): 4.2. Villa Giulia Museum, Rome: 1.3 (right). Special thanks to Nicola Castangia.

Cover design: Julia Kushnirsky
Interior design: Milenda Nan Ok Lee

In memory of Antonietta Boninu, Guido Clemente,

Alessandro Bedini, Paolo Bernardini,

and Mario Torelli

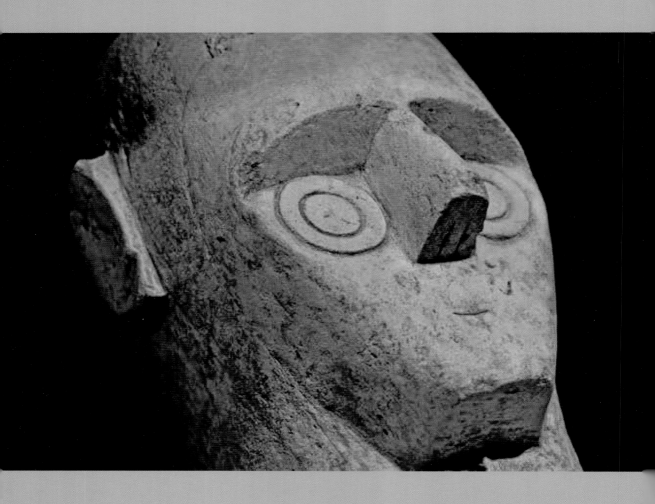

The statuary from Mont'e Prama is notable for its height and for its facial sculpting; this typical figure has a pronounced nose and brow, a small mouth, and eyes symbolized by concentric circles (*Civic Museum of Cabras; Mont'e Prama Foundation*).

Contents

Introduction

BARBARA FAEDDA, Columbia University;
PAOLO CARTA, University of Trento

I T ALL BEGAN in 1974, when fragments of ancient sculptures turned up in a field in western Sardinia. A whole world came to light; dozens of anthropomorphic stone sculptures representing archers, warriors, and boxers, alongside models of *nuraghi* (the prehistoric conical towers of Sardinia) as well as numerous sacred stones known as *baetyls*. Since then, several excavation campaigns have been done, the digging area has expanded, and, little by little, a unique and intriguing history is being revealed to the world here at Mont'e Prama (the "hill of palm trees," in the local language). Meanwhile, the sculptures have been meticulously reassembled by Italian conservators who are global leaders in noninvasive diagnostic techniques and fully reversible treatments that do not alter the objects.

The giant statues—some as tall as 7 feet (2 meters)—and the individual tombs throughout this monumental necropolis make Mont'e Prama uniquely rich in its detailed representation of a culture's values and traditions. At this sanctuary necropolis, high-ranking young men were honored in the same way as the heroes of the past. Military, political, and religious values were conveyed in this sacred space, which symbolized the identity of the society and granted a powerful sense of belonging.

Mont'e Prama is a remarkable example of how islands and insularity shaped the world in ancient times. It gives us the opportunity to delve into the beliefs, values, and practices of a community that lived in the

Mediterranean basin in the Bronze Age and the Iron Age, a period of transition marked by cultural challenges and social developments.

In this volume—commissioned by the International Observatory for Cultural Heritage, conceived within Columbia University's Italian Academy for Advanced Studies—are essays by distinguished scholars in the field of Sardinian and Mediterranean archaeology, experts in restoration and conservation, and a lawyer battling the illicit trafficking of artworks. The book, along with the online digital exhibition that preceded it, are the first initiatives in a multiyear program developed with a grant from Italy's Autonomous Region of Sardinia and designed to highlight Sardinia's cultural heritage.

THE DISCOVERY AND THE EXCAVATIONS

From that first storybook moment in 1974—when farmers unearthed a large anthropomorphic stone head and some archaeological fragments on the Sinis Peninsula, which juts out from the southwestern coastline of Sardinia—Mont'e Prama has seen several excavation campaigns across a widening site.

The Archaeological Superintendency based in nearby Cagliari launched the first dig in 1975, under the direction of archaeologist Alessandro Bedini; this was followed by a series of digs by other distinguished scholars and archaeologists. These yielded a wealth of items: countless heads, arms, legs, and torsos. Along with the giant human figures were found models of baetyls and nuraghi, as well as the base of a temple; within just a few years, dozens of single pit graves had come to light, leading to the determination that a necropolis had been created here in the early period and had been used for many centuries.

A new phase began in the 2000s, when thousands of fragments were transferred to the Conservation and Restoration Center in the city of Sassari, and a team set to work skillfully reassembling the items. Because they were made of a friable limestone, the items were difficult to treat: the experts labored to find the most appropriate restoration methods for this delicate material.

As some teams worked in the laboratory, others sought to understand where the statues were originally placed, and why and how they were later destroyed. Fragments of a single sculpture have been found at quite distant locations. Archaeological stratigraphy showed that the statues were shattered long ago—perhaps they fell on their own, or perhaps they were deliberately destroyed and deposited atop and around the tombs, in which case, by whom and why? These are the questions posed by Alessandro Usai, the archaeologist of the Superintendence of Cagliari and Oristano, who has been directing the research on the site for nearly a decade.

Like much of Sardinia, the Sinis Peninsula is a challenging area because it is fragile and protected. The excavation and study teams have always respected the environment and been careful to not disturb its exceptional vegetation and fauna—they conduct their work so as to preserve the ecological balance of the place. The archaeologists and all the institutions participating in the research also strive to engage the present-day neighbors of Mont'e Prama, leading to a constructive contribution that comes from the involvement of local communities in the larger framework of local, national, and international actors whose common goal is the preservation, study, and enhancement of this invaluable cultural heritage.

THIS BOOK IN CONTEXT AT COLUMBIA UNIVERSITY IN NEW YORK CITY

This book is born of a commitment to the understanding of cultural transmission and the urgent need to preserve all that is meaningful in culture. The concept of heritage is extensive and is frequently modified, reinterpreted, and updated; nonetheless, cultural heritage is widely considered a common ground on which a community's identity is based. The social fabric and the surrounding landscape are also part of cultural heritage.

This volume—like the online digital exhibition that opened in spring 2022 (montepramaexhibition.italianacademy.columbia.edu)—is part of a multiyear program sponsored by the Autonomous Region of Sardinia, which includes a number of projects highlighting Sardinia's cultural heritage, with a particular emphasis on archaeology. This entire program is being developed under the umbrella of the International Observatory for Cultural Heritage.

Conceived in 2016 at the Italian Academy as it marked its twenty-fifth year as a Columbia center for advanced study, the International Observatory is dedicated to all issues relating to the survival, protection, and conservation of cultural heritage. It is historical, practical, and theoretical. It sponsors and encourages research into monuments, artifacts, practices, and traditions. It records losses and destruction of international cultural heritage in all media and across all boundaries and conducts research on treasures at risk—whether from age or location, natural disaster, urban development, conflict, war, or other perils. It is also social, in that it seeks to understand the meaning and value of monuments and objects not only to humanity but also in their local contexts. And it is timely, as it spotlights the political uses and abuses of heritage sites and monuments as well as the exchange, transport, and trafficking of material culture.

Located on the Columbia campus and drawing in part from the expertise of the university's scholars, the observatory has shaped this book and its exhibition so as to introduce the university community (and New York City at large) to the importance of Sardinia in Mediterranean culture. An island marked by cultural contact with outsiders—peaceful contacts as well as invasions by Phoenicians, Carthaginians, Romans, Byzantines, Vandals, and Arabs, and later by Spain and Austria—Sardinia has unknown treasures that merit more study in the United States.

THE ESSAYS

This volume takes the reader through details of the various discoveries at Mont'e Prama, the development of research on the site and its artifacts, the landscape and context, and the meticulous restoration of the items. It ends with a word about the illicit trafficking of Sardinian cultural property.

The iconographies of Mont'e Prama's statuary were established in 1977 by Giovanni Lilliu, the renowned archaeologist and expert on Nuragic civilization, and were confirmed following the restoration of the sculptures. In chapter 1, Raimondo Zucca, a prominent figure in the field of scientific excavations, emphasizes that understanding Mont'e Prama requires clarifying the meaning of the unarmed statues found at the site. Furthermore, toward the end of his chapter, Zucca raises an array of questions: Who was buried in these slab tombs? How did they die? Were they from one single Sardinian lineage? He notes that DNA research now underway may shed light on these issues.

The illuminating chapter by Emerenziana Usai follows. As she directed several excavations at the site starting in the 1970s, she knows every detail of the archaeological work, and thus her essay walks us through the decades of remarkable discoveries by Alessandro Bedini and Giovanni Ugas, by herself, and—in recent months—by Maura Picciau and Alessandro Usai. In this essential chapter can be found every step of the excavation and analysis of the site.

The third essay is a posthumous piece written by the late Guido Clemente for this project at Columbia: Clemente provided an overview of Sardinia's historical and social context at the time when the limestone statues of Mont'e Prama were created. He noted that this site was strategically located along the only route between the sea and the rich mineral deposits inland: the builders had precise goals in mind. They may have blended historical realities with memories of their revered ancestors, thus ennobling themselves as elites who could invoke the magnificent nuraghi to claim power and prestige both within and outside their community.

According to Peter van Dommelen and Alfonso Stiglitz (chapter 4), Mont'e Prama can best be understood if we accept that landscape is socially constituted: that it includes both the physical environment and meaningful places where lives are lived. The authors examine how Iron Age Nuragic people lived in their daily lives; their cultural and commercial contacts with Phoenician and other communities outside of Sardinian shores; and how traces and places reveal their memories and attachments to ancestors during the Iron Age.

Moving from the field to the laboratory, Roberto Nardi, who directs the Archaeological Conservation Center of Rome—which won the prestigious European Union Prize for Cultural Heritage in 2015—opens his essay in chapter 5 by lauding the "titanic work" of a distinguished archaeologist, the late Antonietta Boninu. She brought together regional and national institutions to foster the rebirth of the sculptures, to collect them in a single location, and to make them known to the world. Nardi sketches the puzzles and solutions found as he supervised the restoration of 5,178 fragments, and he describes the synergy between forward-looking public officials and committed conservators in the private sector. Mont'e Prama, he notes, stands as a model for cultural projects.

It is sad to learn that (as Giovanni Lilliu noted) "there are more Nuragic bronzes abroad than there are in Sardinia itself." Giuditta Giardini's essay in the appendix examines the illegal trafficking of Sardinian antiquities, with an overview of the supply chain of tomb robbers, intermediaries, and international dealers. She urges the creation of regional Italian documentation like the "Red Lists" published by the International Council of Museums for other countries with cultural heritage at risk.

THE FUTURE

To our knowledge, this is the first English-language book to address Mont'e Prama's limestone statues, one of the most important archaeological discoveries of the past fifty years. It has been rewarding to introduce these powerful artifacts and their history to new viewers and readers with the initiatives here at Columbia University, and doubly exciting to be doing this in a moment of fresh discoveries. After our team gathered these essays and developed the first public part of the project—the digital exhibition at the Italian Academy—dramatic news began to appear from the Mont'e Prama excavations. Within days of our exhibition going live online, newspapers around the world reported the finding of new statues at the site, described by the Italian culture minister as "two new jewels" that are an "exceptional discovery."

ACKNOWLEDGMENTS

We could not be more grateful to the contributors; their expertise and generosity is unmatched.

We thank the Autonomous Region of Sardinia / Regione Autonoma della Sardegna for its financial support, and the Fondazione Mont'e Prama for its valuable collaboration.

Special thanks are due to the Italian Academy's Director, David Freedberg, and staff—particularly Abigail Asher, Kathleen Cagnina, Aliza Ashraf, Dante Silva, and Rebecca Winterich-Knox. Anita O'Brien provided meticulous editing. We are also grateful to Jane Botsford Johnson, Francesco de Angelis, and Luciana Tocco.

A LOST MEDITERRANEAN CULTURE

CHAPTER ONE

Rites of Initiation, War, and Death in Mont'e Prama

RAIMONDO ZUCCA, University of Sassari

T HE SIGNIFICANCE of Mont'e Prama's forty-four kolossoi and the other sculptures found there is still the subject of lively debate. Much work has been done on the complex since 1974: Gaetano Ranieri's geophysical investigations revealed details about the southern extent of the site southern extent of the site; Alessandro Usai documented this as well, and (from his extensive research) he also wrote essays about the funerary road, the individual shaft tombs, and the dump of statues and nuraghe models.

This essay constitutes an attempt to define the characters of the heroic male statues, which can be subdivided into the armed (warriors and archers) and the unarmed (so-called boxers), to be considered the majority group of initiates, who concluded their initiation time with the bloody athla. These unarmed figures appear to have been led by a group of "military priests," who were the only ones equipped with sandals and an apex, following the model of the Sardinian bronze statuette from Cavalupo (Vulci). The element of braids is also addressed: these were well documented in the statuary of Mont'e Prama and, on the other hand, were very rare in Nuragic bronze male figurines, and absent in female figurines. The figure seems to indicate a characteristic exclusive to the military world, as Giovanni Lilliu intuited.

The idea that the statues of Mont'e Prama attest to bloody games originated from Mario Torelli's formidable perception, developed at the academic conference, *I riti della morte e del culto di Mont'e Prama-Cabras*, held on January 21, 2015:

> The iconography clearly suggests a fundamental opposition between the unarmed and the armed—that is, "boxers" vs. bow- and sword-bearers. Compared to the young men considered eligible to bear arms, the boxers seem to embody intermediate status, of ephebe-like individuals who were, however, already integrated within the group. Their rank, which does not entail the right to bear arms, presupposes the overcoming of a first step of athletic tests revealed by their attributes, the pancratium and the soft leather shield, which distinguished their age class from that of children, who, like the women, were not buried in the sacred necropolis. In particular, to stay within the boundaries of the ancient world, one should think of strongly warlike societies such as Sparta, when imagining what the Nuragic one must have been like. In Sparta, as shown by the classic book by H. Jeanmaire, *Couroi et Courètes, essai sur l'éducation spartiate et star les rites d'adolescence dans l'Antiquité hellénique* (Lille, 1939), the rites of passage following childhood and occurring at each year of age after infancy could be very bloody: one only has to think of those practiced in the sanctuary of Artemis Orthia or in the gymnasium of the Platanistàs— the *athlon* to which these young people were subjected was certainly very bloody. The signs of wounds in the form of cuts and the red coloring of the wounds on the statues are valuable testimony of this need to subject young people to tests to demonstrate their "balentìa."[1]

THE SCULPTURES OF MONT'E PRAMA

The iconological reading of the sculptures of Mont'e Prama proposed by Torelli is therefore based on the opposition between the unarmed (the "boxers") and the armed (the archers/warriors). Giovanni Lilliu made the determination of three iconographies in the statuary of Mont'e Prama in 1977, subsequently reaffirmed them,[2] and reaffirmed them again following the restoration of the sculptures (2007–2011) by the consent of scholars.[3]

Previously, a distinction was postulated between boxers (evoking the sacred *athla*, prize contests) and archers (an expression of the *areté*, military valor).[4] Indeed, a few studies had linked the boxers to the military sphere, and specifically to a sort of sapper, engaged—as a light troop—in actions that would have paved the way for archers and swordsmen.[5]

Regarding the anthropomorphic sculptures as a whole, we currently have the following numbers, still provisional, due to the incompleteness of the reconstruction of the fragments and the archaeological research: forty-four *kolossoi*, of which six are probably equipped with caestus, a rolled shield, sandaled feet, and a conical headdress; eighteen unarmed with armguards and caestus, equipped with a dagger,[6] and a shield worn on the head; eleven archers; and nine warriors.[7] The anthropomorphic sculptures of Mont'e Prama can be attributed stylistically to the so-called Abini group, which is characterized by an acute geometric decorative sense and is also documented in bronzes from northern Sinis.[8] There is no doubt, however, that the Sardinian artisans of Mont'e Prama owed the model of the large statuary to an eastern *artifex*,[9] probably from the North Syrian area,[10] like the later *technitai* of the same milieu who determined the diffusion of large statuary in Casale Marittimo, Ceri, Veii, and Vetulonia in Etruria around 700–650 BCE.[11]

The picture of exchange between the powerful Sardinian communities and the Levantines is clarified by rich archaeological documentation, which demonstrates that access to Sardinian resources—metals in particular—was granted to the Levantines by Sardinian leaders practicing gift exchange, which included eastern techniques and models. Sculpture workshops were at the service of an extraordinary *monumentum* that boldly intended to honor a burial ground with a parade of at least forty *kolossoi* representing male characters with armguards and caestus (called "boxers," as we have seen, but really unarmed figures), archers, and warriors with swords and circular shields.

The Unarmed

The unarmed are characterized by a spheroidal head with a triangular face (round eyes with double circles, a pilaster-like nose, and a mouth barely

FIGURE I.I Sketch and photo of an unarmed figure (*National Archaeological Museum of Cagliari*).

FIGURE I.2 Sandals from an unarmed figure (*Civic Museum of Cabras*).

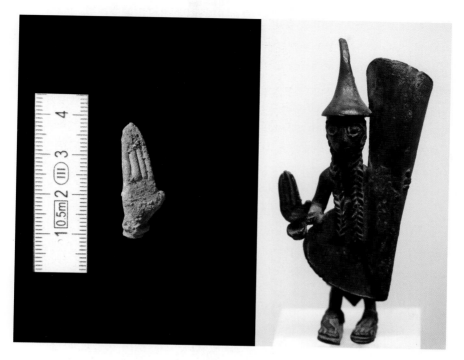

FIGURE 1.3 Similar hands from Mont'e Prama and Cavalupo statues (*left: Cabras; right: Villa Giulia National Archaeological Museum*).

marked by a horizontal or curved incision), grafted with a short neck onto a massive, naked body (apart from a loincloth ending with a point at the back, and a band belt). The genitals appear to be protected by a sheath. The massive lower limbs rest on two broad, bare feet, set on a quadrangular base. The left arm is raised to support the rectangular shield (with rounded corners) above the head. The right arm extends forward, while the forearm, protected by an armguard, is bent vertically, raising a hand sheathed in a caestus, equipped at the top with a short dagger for striking the opponent (figures 1.1, 1.2).

A variant of the iconography of the unarmed with caestus has the right arm lower, with the protected forearm holding the fist within the caestus on the chest, while the left arm supports a rolled-up rectangular shield, with an open flap on the abdomen. The head, equipped in the two known samples with two simple twisted braids, is probably topped by a conical hat. Feet set on a square base wear sandals with sturdy soles.

The discovery in 2014 of the two statues of this type (in one case with the head preserved) was accompanied by the finding of eight sandaled feet, which, together with their intact base—along with a further sandaled foot fragment from the 2017 excavation—suggest the existence in the area of six unarmed statues with caestus, rolled shield, headdress, and sandals. According to Giovanni Ugas these sculptures—"military priests"—participated in a ritual (of initiation) that was structured as a procession marked by the beat of gloved right fists drumming on shields.[12]

This variant is related to the bronze statuette from the necropolis of Cavalupo-Vulci from the second half of the ninth century BCE,[13] representing an unarmed man on whose wrist hangs a caestus; he wears a headdress, sandals, and wrapped shield and raises his right hand in a gesture of prayer. This iconography of the Cavalupo bronze may also be attested in a bronze statuette fragment found in 2017 in Mont'e Prama, consisting of a large right hand, with the thumb spread apart from the other four (extended) fingers in a gesture of prayer; from the end of the forearm that bears a bracelet on the wrist, a caestus could have been suspended, as in the example from Cavalupo (figure 1.3).

Archers

The iconography of the statues is that of the praying archer, standing on a quadrangular base (figure 1.4). The figure has a head protected by a horned helmet, with a triangular face with a pilaster-like nose and round double-circle eyes. The torso is clothed in a tunic that covers the loins. On the chest is a rectangular protective plate, a *kardiophylax*, with straight and concave sides in pairs, pertaining to De Marinis type B,[14] also documented in the Villanovan and Lazio area from 760 BCE[15]—perhaps derived from a neo-Assyrian model.[16] The *kardiophylax* is supported by two pairs of straps that descend from the neck in front and in back to fix the quiver on the shoulders. The left arm, protected by an armguard, enables the gloved hand to support the bow, while the right is bent at a right angle to raise the forearm and the hand, with clenched fingers, in a gesture of prayer. The legs, slightly apart, are grafted with large, unshod feet onto a quadrangular base.

FIGURE 1.4 Sketch and photo of an archer (*National Archaeological Museum of Cagliari*).

Warriors

The warrior has a head with a triangular face with large circular eyes divided by a pilaster-like nose, with a crested cap helmet equipped with two large horns, or with a conical helmet derived from an Assyrian model (figure 1.5).[17] His torso is covered by a tunic with a vertical band, decorated with a pattern of triangles between horizontal lines, ending with fringes. The upper part of the tunic is protected by a plate with large, horizontal segments that seem to extend to the shoulders. The left arm holds a large,

FIGURE 1.5 Sketch and photo of a warrior (*National Archaeological Museum of Cagliari*).

circular shield with a central umbo, while the right hand supports a sword resting on the right shoulder. The lower limbs, probably defended by greaves, rest with bare feet on the usual quadrangular base.

THE INITIATES OF MONT'E PRAMA

As noted, according to Mario Torelli, the anthropomorphic sculptures of Mont'e Prama represent two categories of young males: the unarmed and the armed (the latter further divided into archers and swordsmen).[18] The two categories must refer ideologically to an initiatory progression for the young of the Sardinian lineage society, whose initial stage was to serve unarmed with a shield and caestus, followed by the two stages of the

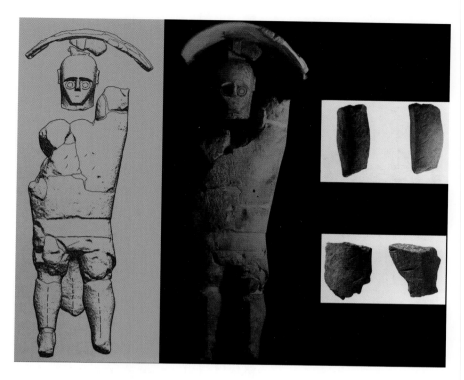

FIGURE 1.6 Sketch and photo of an unarmed man with dagger wounds on his chest and defensive wounds on his lower limbs (*National Archaeological Museum of Cagliari*).

armed—first with a bow and finally with a sword and a circular shield.[19] The unarmed cannot properly be defined as "boxers" since the caestus, with a dagger, is limited to the right hand.[20]

Clarifying the meaning of these unarmed is a fundamental fact, observed by Torelli: wounds appear on the chest and legs of various statues with caestus and shields, characterized by the red color of blood. Medical-forensic analysis of the skin lesions represented on the unarmed of Mont'e Prama suggests stab wounds inflicted on the chest with a blade (dagger), probably as the result of a first-blood clash (the rib cage rendering wounds nonlethal in principle). The wounds on the legs make this interpretation more likely—they are the typical defensive wounds suffered by a fighter when attempting to disarm his opponent by using his lower limbs (figure 1.6).

In Mont'e Prama we therefore have sculptures of unarmed youths (seventeen years old?), initiated into adulthood by means of a bloody *ludus* in

which the opponent is equipped with a dagger; the youths defend themselves with a large shield of soft leather, attacking with the right arm, which
is equipped with an armguard, a hand sheathed in a caestus, and a dagger.[21]
This sanguinary initiation rite was not unlike the scourging of young
Spartans at the altar of Artemis Orthia, which was sprinkled with blood
drawn by the whips: in fact, initiation rituals often involved a particularly
bloody initiatory fight, to prove courage.[22] In time, young men could have
obtained the bow, and finally the sword, which would have marked them as
adult warriors. The Cavalupo type of the unarmed proposes a new theme:
compared to other boxers, this type is characterized by the large, rolled-up
shield, sandals, and, probably, a conical headdress. The other sculptures of
Mont'e Prama have bare feet, as do almost all the bronzes.

We could hypothesize that the unarmed Cavalupo type represents those
of priestly rank (as Lilliu believed about the Cavalupo bronze itself), or the
"best" among the initiates, that is, those who endured the bloody trial most
successfully, such as the βωμονίκας—the victor in the flogging test in front of
the altar of Artemis Orthia.[23]

A second consideration concerns the hair of these sculptures. Since Lilliu's
editio princeps of the sculptural complex, scholars have noticed the particular character of the braids that frame the face and descend to the shoulders
or chest, paralleling the male Nuragic bronzes representing gods with four
arms and two shields, warriors with sword and shield, archers, an unarmed
man praying with sandals and a conical headdress from Cavalupo, praying
priests,[24] and a "peasant" (*bifolco*) with yoked oxen on a Nuragic ship.[25] It
should be noted that most of the Nuragic bronze figurines are characterized by "schematic-branch" hair,[26] which highlights the symbolic value of
the braids—especially characteristic of warriors and archers, but also of the
unarmed Cavalupo bronze statuette.

We cannot exclude the possibility that fashion also played a role, but the
symbolic value of hair (and the shaving of the head) on the stone statue
is documented in ancient sources and in socio-anthropological research.[27]
Lilliu rightly recalled the of Ashtart in Monte Sirai (Carbonia) for the style
of twisted braids that frame the face, a feature that Giovanni Garbini had
ascribed to the North Syrian and neo-Hittite context of the eighth century
BCE.[28] In Mont'e Prama we have the following data on figures with braids:

three out of four warriors, three out of six archers, and ten out of fifteen unarmed men (including the Cavalupo type) have them—in total, sixteen out of twenty-five (64 percent). In Lilliu's corpus on Nuragic bronze sculptures, we have 22 small bronzes of males with braids (15 percent),[29] mainly from the sanctuary of Abini-Teti,[30] compared to 148 male bronze heads without braids, characterized instead by normal schematic-branch hair.[31] The meaning of long hair vs. shaved hair for males has a long interpretative history, starting from Herodotus's account of the battle between Argive and Spartan champions for Thyreae (Hdt. 1.81–83); following their victory, the Spartans resolved to wear their hair long, while the defeated Argives shaved their heads. The ancient interpretation saw the shaving of the Argives' hair as a sign of mourning; moreover, the customs of the Argives and the Spartans were seen as representing the opposition between shaved and long hair that corresponded in substance to the opposition between vanquished = adolescents = inferior, and victors = adults = superior.[32]

Regardless of the problems entailed by initiatory interpretations of this kind—and despite the fact that these interpretations may explain the Herodotean history as the etiological event of an older ritual, also attributed for the Spartans to Lycurgus[33]—we should not exclude the possibility that the choice to represent braids in the Mont'e Prama sculptures instead of short or absent hair may be a symbolic mode for evoking the winners of the bloody trials that signaled the passage between childhood and adulthood.

THE SITE OF THE *ATHLA* OF THE UNARMED AT MONT'E PRAMA

The statues of the unarmed that bear the bloody wounds of the *athla* raise the question of where the initiation trials took place: the sondages of the Soprintendenza in 2016 demonstrated the extension of the archaeological site of Mont'e Prama to the north and south of the 1975–2015 excavation sector, with the continuation of the funerary road and the burial ground, and the existence of a wall in the northwest sector, covered with parallelepiped sandstone blocks, possibly interpretable as a portion of a *temenos*.[34] Archaeological data have so far confirmed the geophysical investigations of Gaetano Ranieri's team, which also identified to the east of the southern

FIGURE 1.7 Aerial view of the site of Mont'e Prama, from the south.

funerary route a resistive anomaly of a semi-elliptical shape that may indicate a festival enclosure space in the sanctuary of Santa Vittoria di Serri.[35] Public acquisition of the areas surrounding the primitive archaeological site of Mont'e Prama will now be necessary for the sake of research and the site's enhancement.

I would like to return to Torelli's clear statement about the existence of a strongly martial society on early Iron Age Sardinia, which was based on the prevalent iconographies of Sardinian bronze statuettes and on the material evidence of swords and spearheads with a related dagger, in bronze and also in iron, in addition to the bronze arrowheads attributable to the ninth and eighth centuries BCE.[36] This claim allows us to overcome recent "all-irenic" theories denying the existence of conflicts among the Sardinian *ethne*, as well as between Sardinians and the many bellicose groups of the Mediterranean world,[37] and is in line with what we know about power relationships as they are generally documented in ancient societies. The community that created the *kolossoi* of Mont'e Prama is therefore a warlike society that narrates through sculpture a Sardinian myth of young heroes who progressed, through a strict education in pain and victory in the bloody *athla*, toward the two armed ranks—archers and warriors with a sword and round shield.

THE NURAGHE AND BAETYL MODELS

The anthropomorphic statues in Mont'e Prama are joined by the limestone and sandstone baetyls, heirs of the Middle and Late Bronze Age rituals that were centered on the ancestor cult in the exedra of the tombs of the Giants,[38] and by the models of single-towered, multilobed (tri-lobed and above all quadri-lobed and octa-lobed) nuraghi in limestone (rarely in sandstone; see figure 1.8). The latter are comparable in part to the lithic nuraghe models belonging to the broader category of architectural models that is also known from the Egyptian, Near and Middle Eastern, Anatolian, Cypriot, Cretan, Mycenaean, and Greek areas,[39] thanks to Béatrice Muller's studies on the *Maquettes antiques d'Orient*.[40] Some of these cases may have provided the inspiration for the nuraghe models. On the other hand, we have rich documentation of architectural maquettes of complex fortified structures, such as the Middle Elamite ones of Tchoga Zanbil (thirteenth century BCE), the recent Bronze Age on Megiddo, from Iron Age I or II, and, probably, in Urartu.[41]

The sculptural complex, built in a single moment, coeval to the monumentalization of the funerary area of Mont'e Prama, poses numerous questions. The burial depositions began on the plain beneath the eastern slope of Mont'e Prama, during Final Bronze Age 3 (eleventh to tenth century BCE?) with the single-deceased burial rite inside a circular pit tomb with roofing stones, which might in fact have been a small tomb rearranged after the monumentalization of the earlier funerary area, which had partially damaged the oldest wells.[42] Burial at the site of the sacred necropolis was reserved for youths and young male adults (remains of an individual found there have been attributed to a female on an anthropological basis, but they need to undergo a DNA test for confirmation). To date, through archaeological investigations (1975–2022) and the excavation tests of the

FIGURE 1.8 Two models of four-lobed nuraghi (*National Archaeological Museum of Cagliari*).

Soprintendenza Archeologia (2016), the Final Bronze Age 3 pit tombs have been determined to extend NNE–SSW for 135.50 m, and to the east for 4 m in width.[43]

In 1975 Alessandro Bedini had identified a circular shaft tomb on the western side of the funerary road of the same type as those discovered on the eastern side in 2017; it is exceptional, according to our state of knowledge. It was excavated on the limestone crust and structured with a basalt and limestone road bed, little preserved, but clearly marked by wagon-wheel furrows: it is 5 m wide, and the presumed length was at least 150 m, based on the geophysical investigations of Gaetano Ranieri.[44]

It should be noted that the excavation in 2017 clarified the existence of a ramp (5 m wide), located in what was probably the middle of the funerary road, which provided access on the eastern side. It was probably opposed to a second ramp on the western slope, pertaining to the circular

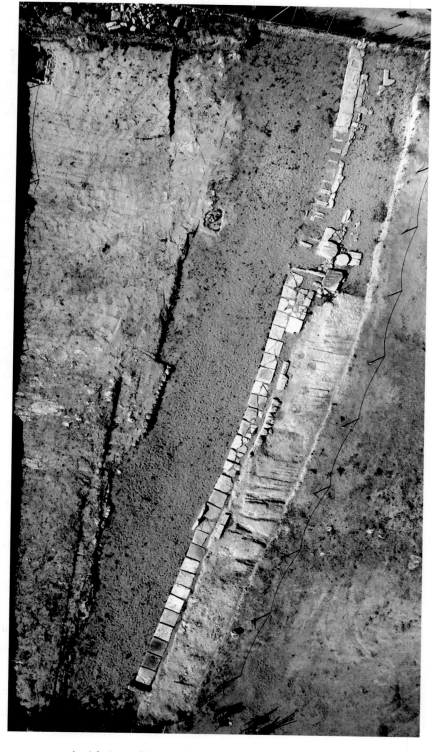

FIGURE 1.9 Aerial view of the tombs of Mont'e Prama.

hut and the adjacent ceremonial rooms,[45] and possibly the other structures (a caisson with ritual offerings, to the west of the Bedini necropolis to the west of the road).[46] Bordered by the great *temenos* wall, perhaps it was completely lined on the eastern side by rectangular blocks of sandstone that were held together by clamps and were meant to stem the waters of the rivulets of Mont'e Prama.[47] The ramp probably connected to a small road that branched off from the main north-south road between the Nuragic settlements of Tharros and Cornus, which was near the limestone quarries used for the sculptural complex of Mont'e Prama.

The eastern ramp had destroyed numerous pit tombs of the Final Bronze Age 3, demonstrating its connection—together with the road—to the second phase of the funerary area's monumentalization, to which we ascribe the easternmost row of pit tombs, covered with (sometimes double) sandstone slabs, and the entire sculptural complex (ninth century to first half of eighth century BCE). The identified slab tombs (preserved or lost) equal perhaps eighty, of which at least twenty-three come from the necropolises discovered by Bedini (1975) and A. Usai (2015–2016), thirty in C. Tronchetti (1977, 1979), eight and three (violated in ancient times) from the necropolis of the 2014 and 2017 excavations, respectively, and an indeterminate number (perhaps twenty) from the area covered by the southern sondages of 2016.[48] The centrality of the ramp descending to the funerary road and of the structures excavated in 1979 and 2015–2016 suggests an equivalence between the slab tombs to the north and south of the ramp. Based on the current state of research, therefore, we can surmise the existence of at least fifty tombs both to the north and to the south of the space without slab tombs, between the southern boundary slab of the Tronchetti tombs and the northern boundary slab of the tombs of 2014 and 2017—an area 10 m wide, in the center of which the ramp was excavated. The anomalies identified in Ranieri's geophysical survey, south of the area corresponding to map 1588 (sheet 8, municipality of Cabras), owned by the Archbishopric of Oristano, and similar to those highlighted in relation to the slab tombs of 2014, lead to the estimate of a hundred slab tombs in the funerary area of Mont'e Prama, approximated by default.

Who are the deceased in the slab tombs? What were the causes of their deaths? Burial in the slab graves was clearly reserved for a group of male individuals, youths (seventeen years old) or young adults: Did they belong to the same gentilicial group, or were they of different Sardinian lineages? These questions require further investigations, such as those already initiated by Salvatore Rubino,[49] divided into separate databases relating to (a) at least three C-14 datings recalibrated for each deceased, since for now the C-14 dates are partially contradictory;[50] (b) the extraction of the DNA of each deceased, to determine the gender and any family ties; and (c) the paleopathological examinations and those concerning the causes of death. This research will shed light on the issue of the shrine of the unarmed and the warriors of Mont'e Prama, as represented in the anthropomorphic sculptures and in the different nuraghe models, which seem to postulate individuals coming from different Nuragic areas.

Translated by Jane Botsford Johnson and Francesco de Angelis

NOTES

1. M. Torelli, "Conclusioni," in *I riti della morte e del culto di Monte Prama-Cabras*, ed. M. Torelli (a cura di), Atti dei Convegni Lincei 303, Accademia dei Lincei (Rome, 2016), 184–85.

2. G. Lilliu, *Dal betilo aniconico alla statuaria nuragica*, in SS 24, 1977–1978, 124–37; G. Lilliu, "La grande statuaria della Sardegna nuragica," in *Memorie dell'Accademia Nazionale dei Lincei* 394, ser. 9, vol. 9, fasc. 3 (Rome 1997), 303–13.

3. M. Rendeli, "Monte'e Prama: 4875 punti interrogativi," in Aa.Vv., *Testo, immagine, comunicazione: immagine come linguaggio*, Atti del XVII Congresso Internazionale di Archeologia Classica (Atti Convegno Roma, 2008), *Bollettino di Archeologia* online 1 (2010): 58–72; R. Zucca, *Per una definizione del complesso archeologico della prima età del ferro di Monte Prama (Cabras–OR)*, Ostraka, Rivista di antichità 21 (2012): 221–61; A. Bedini et al., *Giganti di pietra. Mont'e Prama. L'Heroon che cambia la storia della Sardegna e del Mediterraneo* (Cagliari, 2012); P. Bernardini, "Riflessioni sulla statuaria di Monte Prama," in *Tharros Felix 5*, ed. A. Mastino, P. G. Spanu, and R. Zucca (a cura di) (Rome 2013), 155–98; C. Tronchetti, "La statuaria di Monte Prama nel contesto delle relazioni tra Fenici e Sardi," in *I nuragici, i Fenici e gli altri, Sardegna e Mediterraneo tra Bronzo Finale e Prima Età del Ferro*, ed. P. Bernardini and M. Perra (a cura di) (Sassari, 2012), 181–92; A. Boninu and A. Costanzi Cobau (a cura di), *Le sculture di Mont'e Prama. Conservazione e restauro* (Rome, 2014); M. Minoja and A. Usai (a cura di), *Le sculture di Mont'e Prama. Contesto, scavi e materiali* (Rome, 2014); L. Usai (a cura di), *Le sculture di Mont'e Prama. La mostra*

(Rome, 2014); C. Tronchetti, *Mont'e Prama. L'heroon dei giganti di pietra* (Cagliari, 2015); E. Usai and R. Zucca, *Mont'e Prama (Cabras). Le tombe e le sculture*, Sardegna archeologica, Guide e Itinerari, 57 (Sassari, 2015); G. Ranieri and R. Zucca (a cura di), *Mont'e Prama—I. Ricerche 2014* (Sassari, 2015); P. Bernardini, *Mont'e Prama e i guerrieri di pietra*, Sardegna archeologica, Guide brevi (Sassari, 2016); M. Minoja and A. Usai, "Le sculture nuragiche di Mont'e Prama nel quadro dei rapporti mediterranei della Sardegna dell'età del Ferro," in *Italia tra Mediterraneo ed Europa: mobilità, interazioni e scambi*, ed. M. Bernabò Brea (a cura di) (Rivista di Scienze Preistoriche, 70 S1–2020), 401–10; R. Zucca and G. Paglietti, *I Giganti di Mont'e Prama* (Cabras-OR), ed. Carlo Delfino (Sassari, 2022).

4. C. Tronchetti, "Le tombe e gli eroi. Considerazioni sulla statuaria di Mont'e Prama," in *Il Mediterraneo di Herakles. Studi e ricerche*, ed. P. Bernardini and R. Zucca (a cura di) (Rome, 2005), 145–67.

5. Rendeli, "Monte 'e Prama: 4875 punti interrogativi," 68.

6. G. Paglietti, "Una lama nel buio. Nuova luce sui 'Pugilatori' di Mont'e Prama," *Tharros Felix* 7, Florence c.s.

7. Zucca and Paglietti, *I Giganti di Mont'e Prama*.

8. A. Meloni and R. Zucca, "Nuovi bronzi nuragici da Othoca e dal Campidano settentrionale," *Analysis Archaeologica* 1 (2015): 172–84.

9. Lillu, "La grande statuaria della Sardegna nuragica," 348; Bedini et al., *Giganti di pietra. Mont'e Prama*, 105–34.

10. Rendeli, "Monte 'e Prama: 4875 punti interrogativi," 67 n. 25.

11. A. Maggiani, in Aa.Vv., *Principi etruschi tra Mediterraneo e Europa* (Venezia, 2000), 126–27; G. Colonna and F. von Hase, "Alle origini della statuaria etrusca: la tomba delle statue presso Ceri," *Studi Etruschi* 52 (1986): 13–59; I. Strøm, "Conclusioni," in *Le necropoli arcaiche di Veio. Giornata di studio in memoria di Massimo Pallottino*, ed. G. Bartoloni (Rome, 1997), 245–47; L. Pagnini, in Aa.Vv., *Principi etruschi tra Mediterraneo e Europa*, 128.

12. G. Ugas, "The warriors of Mont'e Prama and the sound of oblong shields," in *Sulle sponde del Tirreno*, ed. F. Cordano and G. Brioschi, "Writings of Archeology in memory of Alessandro Bedini," *ARISTONOTHOS. Review of Studies on the Ancient Mediterranean*, Quaderni n. 7, Milan 2021, 195–221.

13. M. L. Arancio, A. M. Moretti Sgubini, and E. Pellegrini, "Corredi funerari femminili di rango a Vulci nella prima età del ferro: il caso della Tomba dei Bronzetti sardi," in *L'alba dell'Etruria. Fenomeni di continuità e trasformazione nei secoli XII–VIII a.C. Ricerche e scavi*, ed. N. Negroni Catacchio, Atti del IX Incontro di Studi (Milan, 2010), 169–214.

14. G. De Marinis, "Pettorali metallici a scopo difensivo nel villanoviano recente," in *Atti e Memorie dell'Accademia La Colombaria XLI* (1976), 1–30.

15. M. Martinelli, *La lancia, la spada, il cavallo. Il fenomeno guerra nell'Etruria e nell'Italia centrale tra età del bronzo ed età del ferro* (Florence, 2004), 67–71.

16. J. Weidig, *Bazzano—ein Gräberfeld bei L'Aquila (Abruzzen). Die Bestattungen des 8.-5. Jahrhunderts v. Chr. Untersuchungen zu Chronologie, Bestattungs Bräuchen und sozialstrukturen*

im Apenninischen Mittelitalien, Monographien des Römisch-Germanischen Zentralmu-seums, Band 112, 1 (Mainz, 2014), 49–55 n. 5; R. Zucca, *Modelli orientali nei guerrieri in bronzo e pietra della Sardegna tra IX e VIII sec. a. C.*, in Cordano and Brioschi, *Sulle sponde del Tirreno*, 237–61.

17. Zucca, *Modelli orientali nei guerrieri in bronzo*, 238–41, 246–47.

18. Torelli, "Conclusioni," 184–85.

19. E. Franchi, "Riti di iniziazione in Grecia antica? Un terreno d'indagine interdisci-plinare," in *Dalla nascita alla morte: antropologia e archeologia a confronto*, ed. V. Nizzo, Atti dell'Incontro Internazionale di studi in onore di Claude Lévi-Strauss, Atti Convegno Roma 2010 (Rome, 2011), 553–61; R. Zucca, "Sangre y arena nella prima età del Ferro a Mont'e Prama (Sardegna)," in *Dialogando: studi in onore di Mario Torelli*, ed. C. Masseria and E. Marroni (a cura di), MOUSAI. Laboratorio di archeologia e storia delle arti, 4 (Rome 2017), 449–58.

20. Paglietti, "Una lama nel buio."

21. Paglietti, "Una lama nel buio."

22. A. Brelich, *Paides e parthenoi* (a cura di), ed. A. Alessandri and C. Cremonesi (Rome, 2013), 129–228.

23. Brelich, *Paides e parthenoi*, 151.

24. G. Lilliu, *Sculture della Sardegna nuragica* (Cagliari, 1966), 23–24; Lillu, "La grande statuaria della Sardegna nuragica," 308–9 nn. 110–15.

25. Lilliu, *Sculture della Sardegna nuragica*, 401–3 n. 281.

26. Lilliu, *Sculture della Sardegna nuragica*, 23.

27. Lilliu, *Sculture della Sardegna nuragica*, 210.

28. Lilliu, "La grande statuaria della Sardegna nuragica."

29. Lilliu, *Sculture della Sardegna nuragica*, 228, 255; E. Alba, *La donna nuragica. Studio della bronzistica figurata* (Rome, 2005), 86.

30. Lilliu, *Sculture della Sardegna nuragica*, nos. 88–90, 93–94, 96, 100–102, 106, 109–12, 115–16, 118–19, 127–28, 146, 289.

31. Lilliu, *Sculture della Sardegna nuragica*, 23.

32. E. Franchi, *Spartani dalle lunghe chiome e Argivi rasati. Interpretazioni iniziatiche moderne e costruzioni di senso antiche*, Incidenza dell'Antico, 7 (Naples, 2009), 61.

33. A. Brelich, *Guerre, agoni e culti nella Grecia arcaica* (Bonn, 1961); E. B. Harrison, "Greek Sculptured Coiffures and Ritual Haircuts," in *Early Greek Cult Practice*, ed. R. Hägg, N. Marinatos, and J. G. C. Nordquist (Stockholm, 1988), 247–54; D. D. Leitao, "Adolescent Hair-Growing and Hair-Cutting Rituals in Ancient Greece: A Sociological Approach," in *Initiation in Ancient Greek Rituals and Narratives*, ed. D. B. Dodd and C. A. Faraone (New York, 2003), 109–28; E. Franchi, "Comunicare con le chiome: la Battaglia dei Campioni e la social memory spartana," in *La comunicazione nella storia antica: fantasie e realtà*, ed. M. G. Angeli Bertinelli and A. Donati (Genoa, 2008), 237–41; Franchi, *Spartani dalle lunghe chiome e Argivi rasati*, 61–88.

34. A. Usai, "Primi saggi di scavo archeologico nei terreni privati a Mont'e Prama," in *Notizie & Scavi della Sardegna nuragica*, ed. G. Paglietti, F. Porcedda, and S. A. Gaviano (Dolianova, 2020), 358–67.

35. Ranieri and Zucca, *Mont'e Prama—I. Ricerche 2014*.

36. Torelli, "Conclusioni."

37. R. Cicilloni, "Le armi," in *L'isola delle torri. Giovanni Lilliu e la Sardegna nuragica*, ed. M. Minoja, G. Salis, and L. Usai (a cura di) (Sassari, 2016).

38. E. Usai, "Idoli betilici di Mont'e Prama," in Minoja and Usai, *Le sculture di Mont'e Prama*, 293–314.

39. F. Campus and V. Leonelli (a cura di), *Simbolo di un simbolo. I modelli di nuraghe* (Monteriggioni, 2012); V. Leonelli, "I modelli di nuraghe e altri elementi scultorei di Mont'e Prama," in Minoja and Usai, *Le sculture di Mont'e Prama*, 263–92.

40. B. Muller, *Les "maquettes architecturales" du Proche-Orient ancien. Mésopotamie, Syrie, Palestine du IIIe au milieu du Ier millénaire avo 1.C.* (BAH 160) (Beirut, 2002); B. Muller, *Maquettes antiques d'Orient. De l'image d'architecture au symbole* (Paris, 2016).

41. Muller, *Maquettes antiques d'Orient*.

42. A. Usai, "Il primo nucleo monumentale della necropoli di Mont'e Prama," *Quaderni. Soprintendenza Archeologica per le province di Cagliari e Oristano* 31 (2020): 85–108.

43. A. Usai, "Mont'e Prama 2015. Nota Preliminare," *Quaderni. Soprintendenza Archeologica per le province di Cagliari e Oristano* 26 (2015): 75–111; A. Usai, "Il primo nucleo monumentale della necropoli di Mont'e Prama"; A. Usai et al., "Nuovi dati e nuove osservazioni sul complesso di Mont'e Prama (scavi 2015–2016)," *Quaderni, Soprintendenza archeologica per le province di Cagliari e Oristano* 29 (2018): 149–91; A. Usai, "Il primo nucleo monumentale della necropoli di Mont'e Prama"; A. Usai, "Mont'e Prama: le tombe, le sculture, la gente," *Archeologika* 2021, Un'isola di storie antiche, https://monteprama.it/archeologika-2021/.

44. Ranieri and Zucca, *Mont'e Prama—I. Ricerche 2014*.

45. A. Usai and S. Vidili, "Gli edifici A-B di Mont'e Prama (Scavo 2015)," *Quaderni. Soprintendenza Archeologica per le province di Cagliari e Oristano* 27 (2016): 253–92; A. Usai, S. Vidili, and C. Del Vais, "Il settore nordovest e i materiali dell'edificio A di Mont'e Prama (scavi 2015–2016)," *Quaderni, Soprintendenza archeologica per le province di Cagliari e Oristano* 28 (2017): 149–91; A. Usai et al., "Nuovi dati e nuove osservazioni sul complesso di Mont'e Prama (scavi 2015–2016)," 98–110.

46. A. Usai et al., "Nuovi dati e nuove osservazioni sul complesso di Mont'e Prama (scavi 2015–2016)," 94–97.

47. A. Usai, "Mont'e Prama: le tombe, le sculture, la gente."

48. A. Usai, "Primi saggi di scavo archeologico nei terreni privati a Mont'e Prama."

49. S. Rubino, G. Carenti, E. Sias, B. Panico, and R. Zucca, "Identità biologica e identità culturale dei morti di Mont'e Prama (Cabras OR)," in *Archeologia e Antropologia della Morte*, ed. V. Zisso (Rome, 2016).

50. A. Usai et al., "Nuovi dati e nuove osservazioni sul complesso di Mont'e Prama", *Quaderni. Rivista di Archeologia* 29 (2018): 91, 93, tab. I II.

CHAPTER TWO

Mont'e Prama Excavation, Research, and Restoration

EMERENZIANA USAI, Superintendency of Archaeology, Fine Arts and Landscape for the Metropolitan City of Cagliari and Provinces of Oristano and South Sardinia

THE HISTORY of studies and research in Mont'e Prama is almost fifty years old; it began with a chance discovery, brief investigations, and prolonged scientific excavations. It is an extraordinary story. The protagonists are many, but the most famous and seductive are, of course, the large limestone statues of young men—warriors with shields and swords, archers, and unarmed "boxers," more than two meters high. Commonly called "the Giants," they constitute the most important legacy that the late Nuragic communities of Sardinia in the late Bronze and early Iron Ages (1150–900 BCE) left to the island and to the whole world. They communicated much in ancient times, and even today they contribute to making Sardinia and its ancient history known.

The exact number of sculptures is not yet known. So far, there are forty-four limestone anthropomorphic sculptures; thirty-one nuraghe models, thirty-seven of which are in limestone and two in sandstone; and twenty-two baetyls, fourteen of which are in sandstone and five in limestone. These grandiose sculptures date back to the Iron Age (900–700 BCE), glorify military and religious values, and claim the inheritance, lineage, and hegemonic position of the ancestor heroes who built the nuraghi, manifesting a need for celebration, self-representation, and social exaltation. The sculptures were sited in central western Sardinia, in Mont'e Prama, on a large plain in the Sinis di Cabras. Once rich in dwarf palms—hence the name—there was a large sacred necropolis, consisting of individual pit tombs monumentalized in the Iron Age with the erection of anthropomorphic sculptures accompanied by nuraghe models and baetyls.

DISCOVERY (1974)

The exceptional discovery took place when a farmer was plowing the land owned by the Confraternita del Rosario di Cabras, on March 28; he found a large head and other stone sculptural fragments. He immediately notified the Centro di cultura di Cabras, along with Giuseppe Atzori, the honorary inspector of the area, who reported the discovery to the Soprintendenza Archeologica for prompt recovery of the materials: four stone torsos, a head, and two capitals shaped as a nuraghe terrace.

RESEARCH AND STUDIES

Bedini 1975

The first scientific excavation in the Mont'e Prama area was carried out by the Soprintendenza Archeologica di Cagliari e Oristano, following a report of clandestine excavations in November 1975, in the area where the fragments of the sculptures had been found in 1974. Superintendent Ferruccio Barreca instructed Alessandro Bedini, then a young inspector, to intervene immediately. The brief excavation campaign took place between December 3 and 16, 1975, following inspections and cartographic and cadastral research carried out by Bedini and by Giovanni Ugas. Bedini opened a north/south-oriented trench measuring 5 m wide and 12 m long and revealed, for the first time in Sardinia, a Nuragic funerary area consisting of individual inhumation tombs.

Bedini's investigation brought to light a small part of a late Bronze and early Iron Age necropolis with pit tombs, of which seventeen have a simple pit covered with small stones, with a diameter of 50–60 cm and a depth of 60 cm, and twelve have an 80-cm-deep pit covered by a small square sandstone slab. In each tomb the deceased was seated huddled up and without grave goods, except for a few incomplete Nuragic ceramic finds located in some pit tombs without a cover plate. Inspector Bedini's transfer to Florence temporarily halted his brief but fundamental investigations, which he eventually published in the 2000s.[1]

Lilliu 1977

Mont'e Prama continued to attract attention, and in August 1976 Giovanni Lilliu wrote an article in the newspaper *L'Unione Sarda* entitled "On the Dawn of Medicine in Sardinia." In it he linked the stone sculptures to Nuragic bronze statuettes, considering them representations of ancestor heroes connected to a Nuragic quadrangular temple, interpreted as a sanctuary of the plain—perhaps one of the temples (*fana*) of Iolaus, guide to the Thespiades in Sardinia, according to the ancient mytho-historical tradition (Aristotle).

Meanwhile, Lilliu was completing a study that led from the aniconic baetyls to the anthropomorphic stone statuary of Mont'e Prama. In this study he published some fragmentary sculptures found in 1974 and the materials he found on January 4 and 8, 1977: an archer's torso, a head, and other fragments. He assigned the anthropomorphic sculptures to a sanctuary context and attributed them to the most advanced phase of Nuragic civilization, due to the affinity with votive bronze statuettes.[2]

RECOVERY, GUARDIA DI FINANZA, NOVEMBER 1977

On November 1, Raimondo Zucca, then twenty-three years old, saw a tractor on the ground where the sculptures had been found while he was returning from the sea. He alerted Giuseppe Pau, the curator of the Arborense Antiquarium and honorary inspector, who in turn informed the Soprintendenza and the Guardia di Finanza. They immediately carried out an inspection and saw that the tractor had brought two statue busts to light, which the Finanza and Pau recovered.

EXCAVATIONS

Tronchetti–Ceruti 1977: Studies

Carlo Tronchetti, for the Soprintendenza, and Maria Luisa Ferrarese Ceruti, for the Università di Cagliari, conducted research in Mont'e Prama for the first three weeks of December. The investigation involved two trenches: the first in the area of the findings from the previous November, and the second in the southern sector. The results of this short campaign were excellent, thanks not only to the discovery of twelve headless torsos, three heads, a base with foot, numerous fragments of lower and upper limbs, arches, and capitals, but above all to the identification of a sequence of sandstone slabs arranged along the north-south axis, interpreted as the base of a temple. A brief sondage was carried out in the structure, which was defined as a Nuragic hut. The results were promptly published.[3]

Tronchetti 1979: Studies

The 1977 results led the Soprintendenza to plan a large excavation campaign, obtaining funds from the 1979 budget of the Ministero per i Beni culturali e ambientali. With this funding, archaeological investigation could be carried out in Mont'e Prama from July 2 to October 12, 1979. The campaign was directed by Carlo Tronchetti, with Emerenziana Usai, Paolo Bernardini, and Raimondo Zucca. Thirty individual pit tombs were brought to light, covered by square slabs of sandstone with sides from 80 to 100 cm, between 11 and 22 cm thick, placed side by side. The tombs, arranged along the NNE-SSW axis—flanked on the east by four similar tombs, one of which lacked a slab—extended for 35 m and were aligned with the row of graves covered by the square sandstone slabs of the Bedini excavation.

The pits, dug into the limestone layer, are circular or subcircular in shape, with diameters from 50 to 82 cm, and depths between 75 and 85 cm. Below the mouth, the pits tend to widen and then taper toward the bottom, where there is a decentralized dimple of varying size. The deceased was seated or curled up, without grave goods, with a sandstone slab covering his head. Tomb 25 was the only one to include grave goods, consisting of a necklace made up of small bronze beads, a rock crystal pearl, and a scarab seal of glazed steatite of Egyptian or Levantine production.

A strip of beaten limestone soil that was found to the west of the tombs has been interpreted as a road flanking the necropolis. In this space and on top of the tombs, about five thousand sculptural fragments pertaining to statues, nuraghe models, and baetyls were found. All these elements appeared randomly piled up, as if to constitute a dump, probably formed in one or more moments. The last is presumed to have occurred in the Punic age, as indicated by ceramic fragments from the end of the fourth century BCE, recovered at the base of the heap of materials.

The excavation brought to light the row of sandstone slabs delimited to the west by cut slabs. The nuraghe models and the baetyls were created for the monumentalization of the slab-covered pit tombs. The identification as baetyls of those finds that had at first been interpreted as columns allowed the excavators to rule out the hypothesis of a temple building with columns and capitals. The discovery of statue fragments on top of the covering slabs of the tombs, nuraghe models, and baetyls, the latter almost defining sectors of the necropolis and forming its monumental apparatus, and the massing of the fragments in the street no more than 2 m away from the tombs led to the hypothesis that the statues, the nuraghe models, and the baetyls were in close relationship with the necropolis, created for burial and at the same time for sacred use.

Carlo Tronchetti presented the excavation of 1979 in the excavations and discoveries section of *Studi Etruschi* in 1981, in the catalog of the Milanese exhibition on Nuragic civilization, in the proceedings of a conference held in Boston, and in the volume *I Sardi*.[4] With Paolo Bernardini, Tronchetti presented an important study with the emblematic title *L'effigie*,[5] and, with other scholars, a preliminary study of the anthropological analyses of the inhumed in the individual tombs of Mont'e Prama.[6] Osteological analyses on twenty-eight buried subjects determined the prevalence of males, no older than twenty-five years, none of whom were infants.

The bones from Tronchetti's 1979 excavation and Bedini's 1975 excavation, belonging to forty-one individuals, were further investigated in more recent years.[7] The deceased are predominantly male, robust young people, and accustomed to functional overload, probably due to an aptitude for combat and/or the heroic ideal associated with athletic competitions; infants and older people are absent.

Biochemical analyses on the bones of thirty-nine individuals provided data on the diet of one sample of the group. Radiocarbon analyses were carried out on the osteological remains from three of the excavated burials in order to define the chronology; these analyses offer 2 sigma–calibrated datings, which seem to confirm the evidence of the stratigraphic data. East of the slab tombs, a simple pit burial (tomb 8), covered only by small stones—excavated by Bedini—yielded a dating between 1089 and 900 BCE; burials 1 and 20 of the slab-covered tombs from the Tronchetti excavation date to the Iron Age.[8] The dating of the more recent tombs of Mont'e Prama—and, consequently, of the sculptures—between the second half of the ninth century and the first decades of the eighth is corroborated by the comparison of the stone statues with the Nuragic bronze statuettes,[9] confirmed in subsequent studies.[10]

Tronchetti's excavations have defined the characteristics of the sanctuary-necropolis of Mont'e Prama,[11] which was transformed into a heroon (a temple dedicated to a hero) where the high-ranking young deceased of the community were honored as the ancient heroes of the past.[12]

MATERIALS RESTORATION 2007–2011: EXHIBITIONS AND STUDIES

After the excavation in 1979, research was no longer carried out on the site. Tronchetti oversaw the presentation of some sculptures from Mont'e Prama in national and international exhibitions (Karlsruhe, Stockholm, Brussels, Athens, Rome, and Milan). He also curated the exhibition of some sculptures that came to light in 1979, alongside the most important finds identified in 1974 and 1977, in the new Cittadella dei Musei (1993) in Cagliari.

Lack of funding prevented the restoration of the 5,178 sculptural fragments found in Mont'e Prama, which were deposited in the warehouses of the Museo di Cagliari. In 2005 the fragments were transferred to the well-equipped Centro di Conservazione e Restauro of Li Punti in Sassari, thanks to a loan for restoration under an agreement between the Ministero per i Beni e le Attività Culturali and the Regione Sardegna.

The restoration was carried out by Roberto Nardi of the Centro di Conservazione Archeologica di Roma, under the scientific direction of Antonietta Boninu and the procedural responsibility of Luisanna Usai.[13] At the end of the restoration work, which lasted from November 2007 to November 2011, an exhibition of the restored statuary complex entitled "La Pietra e gli Eroi. Le sculture restaurate di Mont'e Prama" was organized by the Direzione Regionale dei Beni Culturali e Paesaggistici della Sardegna in the headquarters of the Li Punti Restoration Center, from November 23, 2011, to January 29, 2012.[14]

Twenty-eight anthropomorphic sculptures were restored: sixteen boxers, six archers, six warriors,[15] twelve nuraghe models,[16] and one baetyl.[17] The museums of both Cagliari and Cabras hoped to exhibit the restored statues at their respective locations, the first in its role as the relevant national museum, the second as the natural seat of the statuary complex. On March 22, 2014, forty years after the first discovery, the exhibition *Mont'e Prama 1974–2014* opened in the morning at the National Museum of Cagliari, with twenty-two statues, and in the evening at the Museo Civico "Giovanni Marongiu" of Cabras, with six statues and four nuraghe models.[18] The Soprintendenze of Cagliari and Sassari published three volumes, the result of cooperative work, relating to the context of the excavations and materials, the conservation and restoration, and the exhibition, respectively.[19]

EXCAVATIONS

Soprintendenza archeologica (A. Usai, E. Usai), University of Sassari (R. Zucca, P. Bernardini, P. G. Spanu), and University of Cagliari (G. Ranieri), 2014

Archaeological research in Mont'e Prama resumed in 2014 thanks to the Archeology of Mont'e Prama project, developed by the Universities of Sassari and Cagliari in agreement with the Soprintendenza per i Beni Archeologici di Cagliari e Oristano. As part of a protocol agreement, the new research included a geophysical report, landscape archaeology analysis, and archaeological excavation.

The investigation, launched on May 5, 2014, and concluded in March 2015, was conducted by the Soprintendenza archeologica di Cagliari (A. Usai and E. Usai), the Università di Sassari (R. Zucca, P. Bernardini, P. G. Spanu), and the Università di Cagliari (G. Ranieri). In addition to the students from the Scuola di Specializzazione in Beni Archeologici of the Università di Sassari, four inmates from the Casa Circondariale di Massama joined in, following a prison training course on archaeology and research. Based on the main geophysical anomalies and analyses of aerial and satellite photos, various excavation tests were done (figures 2.1, 2.2, and 2.3).

The most relevant data were acquired in two squares located about 10 meters south of the southern burial ground excavated by Tronchetti in 1979. Sixteen tombs were found in the area, half of which were simple pit tombs covered with stones in the eastern space; the other half, to the west, were covered by slabs. Investigation of the tombs was carried out by archaeologists and bioarchaeologists Gabriele Carenti and Manuela Sias, directed by Salvatore Rubino of the Università di Sassari. Anthropological and paleopathological analyses indicated that the deceased all had a robust build, good muscle tone, and a habit of exertion, and their activities concentrated on actions involving the arms and legs—all characteristics of a vigorous youth likely to have used weapons.[20]

The most striking finding of the 2014 excavation was the recovery of two sculptures whose iconography was so far absent from the site. The statues were found in a good state of preservation, from head to calves; they represent a character who with his right arm—the hand protected by a *caestus* (a glove made of leather straps) with a dagger—touches an elongated and enveloping shield supported by the other arm. The long braids that descend on the sides of the face, the tight garment, and the shoes evident on the sculptures, together with the particular typology of the shield bearer, bring the specimens close to the iconography of the male bronze statuettes of a "boxer" priest from Cavalupo (Vulci), found in a pit tomb with an urn that housed the ashes of a woman, believed to be a Sardinian married to a Villanovan "prince," around 850 BCE.[21] Also relevant is the discovery, next to one of the two sculptures described above, of a low sandstone pillar (cippus) with the relief of a human face surmounted by a sort of crest that looks like the reproduction of a helmet, similar to the cippi of warriors from Ossi and Viddalba.[22]

FIGURE 2.1 The many discoveries of 2014 included two baetyls and a limestone floor.

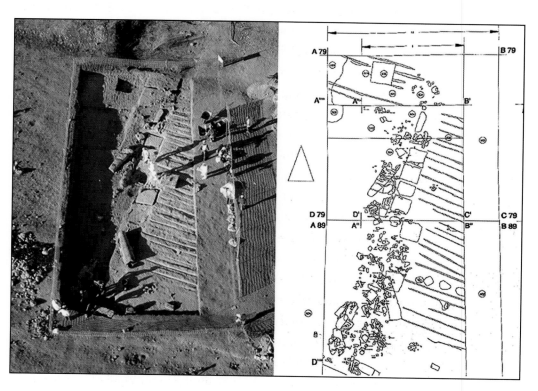

FIGURE 2.2 The baetyls are uncovered in this photo and sketch from 2014, as are two newly found Cavalupo-type boxers.

FIGURE 2.3 Bioarchaeologists working with the archaeologists wore disposable coveralls, headgear, masks, boots, and a double layer of gloves to collect biological samples in the most sterile conditions.

The ceramic finds recovered in the accumulation layer, in association with the sculptural fragments, are partly Nuragic (early Iron Age, around 930–730 BCE), partly Phoenician (seventh to sixth century BCE), and partly Punic (late fourth century BCE), while the Roman-age materials are only in the surface layer. During the 2014 excavation, baetyls were found reaching a height of 2.30 m, among the highest of those identified in Sardinia. The baetyls of Mont'e Prama must be considered unique artifacts, made specifically for the monumentalization of the funerary-sacral area. Along with the nuraghe models, they are important for the interpretation of the entire complex.[23]

To date, Mont'e Prama is the context that has returned the highest number of nuraghe models, which express the symbolic identity value of the nuraghi in an era—the Iron Age—when their construction had long since ceased.[24] The studies of the important excavation campaign in 2014 were published in a volume edited by Gaetano Ranieri and Raimondo Zucca.[25] The volume, with a preface by Mario Torelli, contains numerous works on the history of the studies, the landscape of Mont'e Prama, geotechnologies, the excavation of 2014, material culture documents, and proposals for interpreting the archaeological layering.[26] I would like to highlight specifically landscape archaeology and geophysical studies,[27] as well as those on the C-14 dating of bone samples from two tombs carried out at the Miami laboratory,[28] the excavation of the tombs,[29] and the anthropomorphic sculptures.[30] The definition of the complex and the problems surrounding the destruction of Mont'e Prama are addressed in two studies.[31] The results of the excavations were presented in numerous international conferences and on January 21, 2015, at the prestigious headquarters of the Accademia Nazionale dei Lincei in Rome. The reports were published in a volume entitled *I riti della morte e del culto di Mont'e Prama-Cabras*, with seven essays, respectively, by Mastino and Zucca; Spanu and Panico; Ranieri et al.; A. Usai and E. Usai; Rubino et al.; Bernardini and Zucca; and Mastino, and a preface and conclusions by Mario Torelli.[32]

A. Usai, Studies, 2015–2022

From May 2015 to December 2017, Alessandro Usai, of the Soprintendenza archeologica di Cagliari, with funds from the Società Arcus del Ministero per i Beni e le Attività Culturali e il Turismo, intervened to recover, restore, and expand Bedini's and Tronchetti's trench, which crosses the entire piece of land owned by the Confraternita del Rosario di Cabras from north-northeast to south-southwest. With the excavation campaign of 2015–2016, a large circular Nuragic building, a small adjacent room, and a third room were investigated in the southwestern sector. In the northwest corner of the land, on the slopes of the Mont'e Prama hill, a rectilinear wall made up of basalt blocks and sandstone slabs, about 15 m long and oriented NNW–SSE, shows an orientation toward the buildings named above and probably continues beyond the excavated sector.

The excavation, however, did not provide certain elements to identify functional spaces for any enclosures or links with the necropolis. Sondages on private land to the north, south, and west of the grounds belonging to the Confraternita have shown that to the north, the row of slab-covered tombs and the dump seem to end within 7–8 meters of the northern fence of the archaeological area, while the simple pit tombs, older and without slabs, have been documented up to about 27 m from the same fence. To the south, the complex of tombs seems to end 25–35 m from the fence. In this area there are still simple pit tombs, while those covered with sandstone slabs are not present. Based on the data acquired, the necropolis seems to have a length of 120 m. In September–October 2017, A. Usai and R. Zucca excavated the southern section of the necropolis, investigated in 2014, where the walkway of the funerary road was revealed.

In May 2022 Maura Picciau and Alessandro Usai of the Soprintendenza archeologica di Cagliari, who continued the investigation, discovered two statues depicting boxing priests of the Cavalupo type.[33] Studies of a general nature on Mont'e Prama have not been lacking in recent years.[34] In future investigations, the excavation area will have to be expanded to clarify the relationship of the sanctuary necropolis to any structures, and the possible existence of what is now documented only in the sources and myths. There will be more to come from the site of Mont'e Prama.[35]

Translated by Jane Botsford Johnson and Francesco de Angelis

NOTES

1. A. Bedini, "Gli scavi a Mont'e Prama nel 1975," in *La pietra e gli eroi. Le sculture restaurate di Mont'e Prama*, ed. M. Minoja and A. Usai (Sassari, 2011), 17–20; A. Bedini, "Gli scavi del 1975: l'antefatto" and "Lo scavo," both in *Giganti di Pietra. Monte Prama. L'heroon che cambia la storia della Sardegna e del Mediterraneo*, ed. A. Bedini et al. (Cagliari, 2012), 185–88, 189–206; A. Bedini, "Mont'e Prama. Campagna di scavo dicembre 1975," in *Le sculture di Mont'e Prama. Contesto, scavi e materiali*, ed. M. Minoja and A. Usai (Rome, 2014), 137–54.

2. G. Lilliu, "Dal betilo aniconico alla statuaria nuragica," *Studi Sardi* 24, 1975–77 (Sassari, 1978): 113–44.

3. C. Tronchetti, "Monte Prama (Comune di Cabras-OR)," *Studi Etruschi* 46 (Firenze, 1978): 589–90.

4. C. Tronchetti, "Monte Prama (Comune di Cabras-OR)," *Studi Etruschi* 49 (1981): 525–27; C. Tronchetti, "Nuragic Statuary from Monte Prama," in *Studies in Sardinian Archeology, II: Sardinia in the Mediterranean*, ed. M. S. Balmuth (Ann Arbor: University

of Michigan Press, 1986), 41–59; C. Tronchetti, *I Sardi. Traffici, relazioni e ideologie nella Sardegna arcaica* (Milan, 1988).

5. P. Bernardini and C. Tronchetti, "L'effigie," in AA.VV., *Sardegna preistorica. Nuraghi a Milano* (Milan, 1985), 226–44.

6. C. Tronchetti, F. Mallegni, and F. Bartoli, "Gli inumati di Monte Prama," *Quaderni. Soprintendenza Archeologica per le province di Cagliari e Oristano* 8 (1991) (Cagliari, 1992), 119–31.

7. E. Pacciani and O. Fonzo, "Analisi antropologica dei resti umani della necropoli di Mont'e Prama (Cabras, Oristano)," in *Atti della XLIV Riunione scientifica dell'Istituto Italiano di Preistoria e Protostoria*, vol. 3 (Florence: Comunicazioni, 2012), 1023–29; O. Fonzo and Pacciani, "Gli inumati della necropoli di Mont'e Prama," in Minoja and Usai, *Le sculture di Mont'e Prama*, 175–200; R. Cameriere et al., "L'età dei defunti di Mont'e Prama: un aspetto interessante e cruciale," in Minoja and Usai, *Le sculture di Mont'e Prama*, 201–206.

8. L. Lai et al., "Isotopi stabili e radioattivi: primi dati su dieta e cronologia assoluta delle sepolture di Mont'e Prama," in Minoja and Usai, *Le sculture di Mont'e Prama*, 207–18.

9. G. Lilliu, "Bronzetti e statuaria nella civiltà nuragica," in *Ichnussa, La Sardegna dalle origini all'età classica*, ed. Atzeni et al. (Milan, 1981), 179–254; G. Lilliu, *La grande statuaria nella Sardegna nuragica, Memoria dell'Accademia Nazionale dei Lincei*, 9, 9, 3 (Rome, 1997), 228–388; G. Lilliu, *Sculture della Sardegna nuragica* (Nuoro, 2008).

10. F. Lo Schiavo, "La scultura nuragica, dai bronzi figurati alle statue di Mont'e Prama," in Minoja and Usai, *La pietra e gli eroi*, 35–38; F. Lo Schiavo, "La scultura nuragica dai bronzi figurati alle statue di Mont'e Prama," in Minoja and Usai, *Le sculture di Mont'e Prama*, 99–110.

11. Tronchetti, "Gli scavi del 1977 e 1979: l'antefatto" and "Lo scavo," both in Bedini et al., *Giganti di Pietra*, 207–10, 211–46; C. Tronchetti, "Gli scavi del 1977 e 1979," in Minoja and Usai, *Le sculture di Mont'e Prama*, 155–74.

12. G. Lilliu, "L'oltretomba e gli dei," in *Nur. La misteriosa civiltà dei Sardi*, ed. D. Sanna, (Milan, 1980) 116–20; G. Lilliu, "La civiltà nuragica," in *Sardegna archeologica, Studi e monumenti* 1 (Sassari, 1982), 135–36; C. Tronchetti, "Le tombe e gli eroi. Considerazioni sulla statuaria di Mont'e Prama," in *Il Mediterraneo di Herakles. Studi e ricerche*, ed. P. Bernardini and R. Zucca (Rome, 2005), 145–67; R. Sirigu, *Le tombe degli eroi nella necropoli di Monte Prama*, in Darwin Bimestrale di scienze 1 (Rome, 2006), 40–45; M. Rendeli, "Mont'e Prama: 4985 punti interrogativi," in *Language and Religion. Linguaggio e religione*, ed. M. Dalla Riva, Proceedings of the XVII International Congress of Classical Archeology, *Bollettino di Archeologia* online (Roma, 2010), 58–72; R. Zucca, "Monte Prama e i pedia iolàeia," in AAVV, *Tharros Felix*, vol. 4, ed. A. Mastino and P. G. Spanu (Roma, 2011), 105–18; R. Zucca, "Per una definizione del complesso archeologico della prima età del fero di Monte Prama (Cabras-Or), Ostraka," *Rivista di antichità* 21 (Pisa, 2012), 221–61; P. Bernardini, "Riflessioni sulla statuaria di Monte Prama," in *Tharros Felix 5*,

ed. A. Mastino, P. G. Spanu, and R. Zucca (Rome, 2013), 155–98; Tronchetti, "Gli scavi del 1977 e 1979," in Minoja and Usai, *Le sculture di Mont'e Prama*, 155–74.

13. A. Costanzi Cobau, ed., *Le sculture di Mont'e Prama viste da vicino* (Rome, 2011), 4–32.

14. Minoja and Usai, *La pietra e gli eroi*.

15. L. Usai, "Pugilatori, arcieri e guerrieri," in Minoja and Usai, *La pietra e gli eroi*, 25–30.

16. V. Leonelli, "Rappresentazioni di architettura," in Minoja and Usai, *La pietra e gli eroi*, 21–34.

17. E. Usai, "I betili di Mont'e Prama," in Minoja and Usai, *La pietra e gli eroi*, 39–40.

18. L. Usai, "Le statue nuragiche," 219–62, in Minoja and Usai, *Le sculture di Mont'e Prama*; V. Leonelli, "I modelli di nuraghe e altri elementi scultorei di Mont'e Prama," in Minoja and Usai, *Le sculture di Mont'e Prama*, 263–92; E. Usai, "Idoli betilici di Mont'e Prama," in Minoja and Usai, *Le sculture di Mont'e Prama*, 293–314; L. Usai and V. Leonelli, "Le sculture in mostra," in *Le sculture di Mont'e Prama. La mostra*, ed. L. Usai (Rome, 2014), 235–54.

19. Minoja and Usai, eds. *Le sculture di Mont'e Prama*; A. Boninu and A. Costanzi Cobau, eds., *Le sculture di Mont'e Prama. Conservazione e restauro* (Rome, 2014); L. Usai, ed., *Le sculture di Mont'e Prama. La mostra* (Rome, 2014).

20. G. Carenti, E. Sias, and B. Panico, "Lo scavo delle tombe," in *Mont'e Prama-I ricerche 2014*, ed. G. Ranieri and R. Zucca (Sassari, 2015), 178–84; S. Rubino et al., "Bioarcheologia a Mont'e Prama, in *I riti della morte e del culto di Monte Prama-Cabras*, ed. M. Torelli, Atti dei Convegni Lincei 303, Accademia dei Lincei (Rome, 2016), 101–12; O. Fonzo and E. Pacciani, "Le genti di Mont'e Prama: analisi osteologiche," in *Il tempo dei nuraghi. La Sardegna dal XVIII all'VIII secolo a. C.*, ed. T. Cossu, M. Perra, and A. Usai (a cura di) (Nuoro, 2018), 395–97.

21. F. Caputo, "Pugilatori del tipo Cavalupo," in *Mont'e Prama—I ricerche 2014*, ed. G. Ranieri and R. Zucca (Sassari, 2015), 205–14.

22. F. Lo Schiavo, "Tre guerrieri," in *Studi di antichità in onore di Guglielmo Maetzke* (Archaeologica-49) (Rome, 1984), 67–78; L. Tocco, "Cippo con rappresentazione schematica di guerriero," in Ranieri and Zucca, *Mont'e Prama—I ricerche 2014*, 244–49.

23. E. Usai, "Nuovi idoli betilici a Mont'e Prama," in Ranieri and Zucca, *Mont'e Prama—I ricerche 2014*, 265–69.

24. C. Nocco, "I modelli di nuraghe," in Ranieri and Zucca, *Mont'e Prama—I ricerche 2014*, 254–64.

25. G. Ranieri and R. Zucca, eds., *Mont'e Prama—I ricerche 2014* (Sassari, 2015).

26. M. Torelli, "Prefazione," in Ranieri and Zucca, *Mont'e Prama—I ricerche 2014*, 12–13.

27. B. Panico, and P. G. Spanu, "Archeologia dei paesaggi di Mont'e Prama e del territorio del Sinis," in Ranieri and Zucca, *Mont'e Prama—I ricerche 2014*, 48–57; A. Trogu, F. Loddo, and G. Ranieri, "Il georadar multicanale 'Stream X.' Come vedere nel sottosuolo," in Ranieri and Zucca, *Mont'e Prama—I ricerche 2014*, 86–98.

28. G. Carenti, G. Ranieri, and R. Zucca, "2015 Datazione al c14 di tre campioni ossei delle tombe B/2014 e 7/2014," in Ranieri and Zucca, *Mont'e Prama—I ricerche 2014*, 147–51.

29. G. Carenti, E. Sias, and B. Panico, "Lo scavo delle tombe," in Ranieri and Zucca, *Mont'e Prama—I ricerche 2014*, 178–95; E. Usai and B. Panico, "Mont'e Prama e le sepolture individuali nuragiche," in Ranieri and Zucca, *Mont'e Prama—I ricerche 2014*, 325–36.

30. B. Panico et al., "Pugilatori, arcieri, guerrieri," in Ranieri and Zucca, *Mont'e Prama—I ricerche 2104*, 198–243.

31. P. Bernardini, A. Scarpa, and R. Zucca, "Il problema della definizione del complesso di Mont'e Prama," in Ranieri and Zucca, *Mont'e Prama—I ricerche 2104*, 353–77; L. Tocco, P. Bernardini, and R. Zucca, "La distruzione di Mont'e Prama," 378–88, in Ranieri and Zucca, *Mont'e Prama—I ricerche 2104*, 155–56.

32. A. Mastino and R. Zucca, "Mont'e Prama. Le ragioni e le strategie dello scavo," 15–29; P. G. Spanu and B. Panico, "Archeologia dei paesaggi di Mont'e Prama," 31–47; G. Ranieri et al., "Vedere nel sottosuolo di Mont'e Prama," 49–73; A. Usai and E. Usai, "Mont'e Prama: la morte e il culto nel Sinis dal Bronzo Recente alla Prima Età del Ferro," 75–100; S. Rubino et al., "Bioarcheologia a Mont'e Prama," 101–12; P. Bernardini and R. Zucca, "Lo 'statuto eroico' dell'heroon di Monte Prama," 113–50; A. Mastino, "Aristotele e la natura del tempo: la pratica del sonno terapeutico davanti agli eroi della Sardegnan," 151–78; M. Torelli, "Prefazione," 7–10; and A. Carpinelli, "Premessa," 11–4, all in Torelli, *I riti della morte e del culto di Monte Prama-Cabras*.

33. A. Usai, "Mont'e Prama 2015. Nota Preliminare," *Quaderni. Soprintendenza Archeologica per le province di Cagliari e Oristano* 26 (2015): 75–111; A. Usai and S. Vidili, "Gli edifici A–B di Mont'e Prama (Scavo 2015)," *Quaderni* 27 (2016): 253–92; A. Usai, S. Vidili, and C. Del Vais, "Il settore nordovest e i materiali dell'edificio A di Mont'e Prama (scavi 2015–2016)," *Quaderni* 28 (2017): 149–91; A. Usai et al., "Nuovi dati e nuove osservazioni sul complesso di Mont'e Prama (scavi 2015–2016)," *Quaderni* 29 (2018): 81–140; M. Minoja and A. Usai, "Le sculture nuragiche di Mont'e Prama nel quadro dei rapporti mediterranei della Sardegna dell'età del Ferro," in *Italia tra Mediterraneo ed Europa: mobilità, interazioni e scambi* ed. M. Bernabò Brea (Rivista di Scienze Preistoriche, 70 S1, 2020), 401–10; A. Usai, "Primi saggi di scavo archeologico nei terreni privati a Mont'e Prama," in *Notizie & Scavi della Sardegna nuragica*, ed. G. Paglietti, F. Porcedda, and S. A. Gaviano (Dolianova, 2020), 358–67; A. Usai, "Il primo nucleo monumentale della necropoli di Mont'e Prama," *Quaderni* 31 (2020): 85–108; A. Usai, "Mont'e Prama: le tombe, le sculture, la gente," *Archeologika* (2021), Un'isola di storie antiche, https://monteprama.it /archeologika-2021; M. Minoja and A. Usai, "Le sculture nuragiche di Mont'e Prama nel quadro dei rapporti mediterranei della Sardegna dell'età del Ferro," in *Italia tra Mediterraneo ed Europa: mobilità, interazioni e scambi*, Rivista di Scienze Preistoriche, 70 S1 (2020), ed. M. Bernabò Brea, 401–10, https://www.beniculturali.it/comunicato/archeologia -mic-il-parere-degli-esperti-sui-due-nuovi-giganti-di-monte-prama.

34. C. Tronchetti, *Mont'e Prama. L'heroon dei giganti di pietra* (Cagliari, 2015); P. Bernardini, *Mont'e Prama e i guerrieri di pietra* (Sassari, 2015); E. Usai and R. Zucca, *Le tombe e le sculture* (Sassari, 2015); P. Bernardini and R. Zucca, "Lo 'statuto eroico' dell'heroon di Monte Prama," in Torelli, *I riti della morte e del culto di Monte Prama-Cabras*, 113–50; R. Zucca, "Le statue colossali nuragiche di Mont'e Prama: un giacimento funerario e cultuale," in *La Sardegna nuragica. Storia e monumenti*, ed. A. Moravetti et al., (Sassari, 2017), 291–307; R. Zucca, "Sangre y arena nella prima età del Ferro a Mont'e Prama (Sardegna)," in *Dialogando: Studi in onore di Mario Torelli (MOUSAI)*, ed. C. Masseria, E. Marroni, Laboratorio di archeologia e storia delle arti, 4 (Rome, 2017), 449–58; L. Usai, "L'autorappresentazione: bronzetti e statue," in *Il tempo dei nuraghi. La Sardegna dal XVIII all'VIII secolo a. C.*, ed. T. Cossu, M. Perra, and A. Usai (Nuoro, 2018), 350–75; and A. Usai, "Il complesso funerario e scultoreo di Mont'e Prama," in Cossu, Perra, and Usai, *Il tempo dei nuraghi*, 384–94. See now https://www.beniculturali.it/comunicato /archeologia-mic-il-parere-degli-esperti-sui-due-nuovi-giganti-di-monte-prama.

35. R. Zucca, "Monte Prama (Cabras, Or). Storia della ricerca archeologica e degli studi," in *Tharros Felix* 5, ed. A. Mastino, P. G. Spanu, and R. Zucca (a cura di) (Rome, 2013), 199–286; A. Mastino and R. Zucca. "Storia degli studi," in Ranieri and Zucca, *Mont'e Prama—I ricerche*, 17–28. The Mont'e Prama Foundation was established on July 1, 2021, with the aim of communicating and enhancing the site, the museum, and the entire Sinis region, supported by the MIC, through the Soprintendenza archeologica, the regional secretariat, the regional department of museums, and the municipality of Cabras (https://monteprama.it/).

CHAPTER THREE

Sardinian Society in the Mont'e Prama Era

A Community of Heroes and Warriors

GUIDO CLEMENTE, University of Florence

Introduction by Marco Maiuro, Sapienza University of Rome

G UIDO CLEMENTE, a notable Sardinian ancient historian at the University of Florence, was invited to come to New York to deliver a talk on the society of Mont'e Prama in March 2020. The invitation was inspired by Clemente's interest in the most ancient past of the island, which he had been researching at least since 2010, and concerning which he had already completed a several-hundred-page manuscript that was ready for publication. The invitation had to be canceled because of the pandemic, and then Clemente fell ill in autumn 2020. He died in February 2021.

The text published here was prepared for Clemente's talk. I read it and talked about it with the author, who then amended it after some very fruitful discussion. It lacks footnotes and a bibliography, and I could not find any illustrative slides on Clemente's computer, so the editors have collaborated to add images that may enhance the reader's experience. His family and his widow decided to publish the text as it was written, without further intervention except for polishing the English. I hereby express my gratitude to the Italian Academy, to Professors Paolo Carta and Barbara Faedda for accepting this text, and last but not least to Jane Botsford Johnson for her editing help.

This short piece is valuable because it shows Clemente's best qualities: it is a concise historical analysis of the societies that produced the statues.

A historian accustomed to dealing with written sources, as he was, might not have been attracted to a topic that relies exclusively on nonspeaking objects—architectural remains, artifacts, and statues—but Clemente's ability to meet this challenge is further testimony to his remarkable flexibility. As for the content, his allusions to the Homeric world, though necessarily distant in place and to some extent time, are an excellent starting point for any further discussion of the society of Mont'e Prama. Clemente's forthcoming monograph on the history of Sardinia will shed further light on the nexus between heroic societies, Homeric poems, and the Mediterranean cultural koine.

In the second millennium BCE, Sardinia was the home of a civilization that we call Nuragic. The name comes from the *nuraghi*, or stone buildings in the shape of towers. The Nuragic people were organized in a kind of tribal society, but this does not tell us much, since there are many different tribal societies, clans, or family groups, both small and large, based on kinship and/ or patron-client ties. We do not know enough about their religion, mentality, social structures, or language. But for our purposes, it will be enough to mention some features of this complex civilization. It lasted from around 1600 BCE until the end of the Bronze Age, around the tenth century. After that time, we can detect very big changes, which we can only see in their final stage—we are unable to follow their history in any detail.

We may safely assume that it was a well-organized, centralized society, based on a hierarchy that could command the labor and resources necessary to build the imposing and elaborate nuraghi—not an easy task. This construction presupposes a rather developed technical expertise. Furthermore, such a large number of nuraghi indicates a huge population, and the need to feed it. Population estimates range from 300,000 to 700,000, but even the low figure is impressive for that age. Another feature is now increasingly in the foreground, due to recent research: it was not an isolated society—it had very early contacts with the Near East, Greece, and Cyprus in particular.

The functions of the nuraghi must have been varied. The most elaborate had a large *nuraghe* at the center, usually called the regia, which commanded a vast area with other single nuraghi that were probably watch towers, and stone huts covered with conical straw roofs. They no doubt had a military function, but at the same time they may have been used as storage rooms for food supplies, along with weapons and work instruments for the community, and may also have housed the chief (or chiefs) and his family. The total number of nuraghi is calculated in the range of six thousand to seven thousand, although we do not know whether they were all in use at the same time.

From the ninth to the seventh centuries, some nuraghi were abandoned, while others were destroyed or collapsed due to lack of maintenance. Many still stood, but with a very different, surprising function: they became a kind of sacred place. The nuraghe was no longer the political center of the community, but a center that marked—in some religious way—its identity, rooted in an ancestral past symbolized by these imposing monuments. Around them, literally often in their shadow, people lived in villages. In many, new features appeared: around a square, huts formed a circle. Some huts were probably destined for sacred purposes, like the water cult, and some were organized in a network of small alleys, designed to facilitate the passage of people and goods. The square probably functioned as the center of the community and as a marketplace.

In many villages a larger hut was built, with seats around the wall, and an altar at the center, where a sculpture, a nuraghe model, could be used to perform rites like the burning of offerings. These huts were meeting places where the most important members of the community (or communities) made decisions. It is significant that some of these places were incorporated into the outer walls of the nuraghe; in some instances, nuraghi models were located inside the nuraghe itself, as an altar on one of the inner towers (figures 3.1, 3.2, and 3.3).

This was a major change. It is not easy to give a precise definition of this society because in fact we know very little and can proceed only with great caution while using questionable categories, like comparisons and analogies with contemporary societies we know better, especially in Italy. What we lack is any literary evidence, any continuous history—like Livy's history of Rome—that could answer some basic questions, like the mentality, religious beliefs, and development of this civilization. Archaeology can answer a number of questions, if properly asked, but it cannot answer all of them, and

FIGURES 3.1–3.3 Dozens of models of nuraghi have been found (*Civic Museum of Cabras*).

we must resist the temptation to fill the vacuum by building models that, by presuming too much, end up being abstract. With this in mind, we must proceed with what we have and attempt some reasonable reconstructions based on facts and sound evidence.

The end of the golden age of the nuraghi does not indicate decay—the society that followed was different, but lively and open. The villages were run by some kind of aristocracy, a term we must use loosely to define an elite governing group. This is clear from the existence of the meeting huts. The base for the power of these groups is not easy to define: Were they an elite based on birth or on military expertise and wealth, or both? We know that these villages practiced commerce on a relatively large scale, importing high-quality goods meant to underline the prestige of the leading groups, and exporting minerals and agricultural products. Some places, like Sant'Imbenia in the northwestern corner of the island, produced their own amphorae, to transport goods in fairly large quantities to distant areas of the western Mediterranean, from Spain to Carthage.

Commerce was in fact booming in these centuries, and Sardinia profited from it. Homer vividly describes the merchants of the Iron Age, although from the point of view of the landed aristocracy who despised any commercial activity as low and unbecoming (*Iliad* 23.741ff.; *Odyssey* 14.287–98, 15.415–83). These people arrived in places with safe harbors and built temporary emporia, or marketplaces, where they lived at times for many months, exchanging goods gathered from different markets. The ships may have been Phoenician or Greek, but the crew was mixed, coming from different places. The circulation of goods meant the circulation of people and ideas. The result of these contacts was to pave the way for the meeting of different cultures. Phoenician cities were established along the coasts of southern and central-western Sardinia around the end of the eighth and the seventh centuries. Relations between the newcomers and the local populations were, from what we understand, usually peaceful; merchants did not come in large groups, and they brought gifts and artifacts, probably artisans, and new techniques.

Local communities were receptive but not passive; they had an important past, which was still visible in the landscape in a rather imposing manner. More or less consciously, as is clear from the presence of the nuraghe models and other symbols of this past, they resisted assimilation, taking what was useful and functional for the society they had built on the memory of their own civilization. The new contributed to the old in various ways but did not destroy it.

These remarks are relevant to the striking appearance of the Mont'e Prama compound, on the Sinis peninsula on Sardinia's central-western coast (visible in map 4.1 in the chapter up ahead by van Dommelen and Stiglitz). This was a rich area with natural lagoons and harbors that provided excellent fishing and hunting, and fertile land for agriculture. To the north was Monti Ferru (Iron Mountain), rich in minerals. Between the mountain and the coast, around eight miles from Mont'e Prama, there was a huge nuraghe, S'Urachi, which was probably used into the Iron Age, unlike most others. The Sinis was on the route followed from ancient times by ships traveling from the eastern Mediterranean to Spain, avoiding the dangerous straits between Sicily and peninsular Italy, and the powerful Etruscans firmly established along the Tyrrhenian coast.

In the Bronze Age the Sinis was densely populated; more than one hundred nuraghi have been counted. In the Iron Age, while the majority of the nuraghi were abandoned, the villages grew, some becoming very large; more than forty have been counted. These numbers are approximate since very few have been excavated, but the general picture is credible. Thus the presence in the area of a monument that up to now has no parallel in the western Mediterranean should not really surprise us.

The other chapters in this volume describe in detail, and with the benefit of direct experience in the field, the sculptures, the excavations, and the restoration—a fascinating adventure. For my purposes, it will be enough to describe the monument in its general features, to try to place it in context. It was located along the only route from Monti Ferru to the sea and was clearly a strategic site, designed to convey the idea that the people who built it were in control of the area and had the strength and prestige to claim it. The whole area was a cemetery, in existence for a few centuries, which was enriched with this enormous complex around the middle of the eighth century. This was no longer a mere burial area: it was a monument, formed by a great number of life-size (or even larger) anthropomorphic statues, by nuraghe models, and by baetyls. The statues represented archers, warriors,

FIGURE 3.4 The baetyls were created elsewhere and then brought to the site (*National Archaeological Museum of Cagliari*).

and "boxers," who were unarmed, half-naked, and carried a shield. The nuraghe models described most of the types known, from the single tower to the polylobate. The baetyls are very interesting since they were not made in loco, like the other sculptures, but were brought to the Giants' Tombs, where they usually remained, guarding the entrance (figure 3.4). More than seventy sculptures have been counted, including forty anthropomorphic statues and thirty nuraghe models.

The date, although disputed, should be around the second half of the eighth century, according to a scaraboid found in a tomb, whose typology is precisely dated on the basis of others known in the Near Eastern city of Tyrus in chronologically sound contexts. The Mont'e Prama complex is the first known example of life-size sculptures—earlier than those in Greece by some decades, and much earlier than those in Italy. Naturally the question arises of who made them. What produced such a significant development, from small anthropomorphic statues common in the Mediterranean area to these enormous sculptures, until now present only in the eastern kingdoms? Moreover, what do they tell us about the society, the thoughts, and the culture of the people who produced them?

One feature is immediately evident and of the greatest importance: the anthropomorphic statues copy the small bronze figures (bronzetti), well known and rather common in Sardinia, with great attention to detail; these bronzetti were produced on the island roughly from the tenth century, and, according to some scholars, up to the fifth and even the fourth centuries (figures 3.5, 3.6, and 3.7). They are different in their typology, from the warrior type to the representation of unarmed people carrying animals, probably as offerings to a divinity. Many are in an attitude of devotion, with their hand raised. The chronology of the different typologies is not certain; the ones that inspired the Mont'e Prama sculptures, the warrior type, were most probably among the oldest.

We have a striking comparison in the bronzetto found in a tomb at Vulci, in ancient Etruria, dated at the turn of the ninth century. A sculpture recently found in Mont'e Prama reproduces it in every detail (the sandal, the shield in a vertical position, the headdress); this tells us the age of the typology of these bronzetti and that the artisans who made them used the different models available, not as a loose generic inspiration, but to reproduce something precisely for some reason. The statues show some iconographic details typical of Near Eastern iconography; it is impossible to determine whether this means that the artisans came from that region, or whether local artisans introduced these elements after learning about them from newcomers. The inspiration is completely local; these people wanted to describe their society, rooted in the past, but lively and receptive to different cultures.

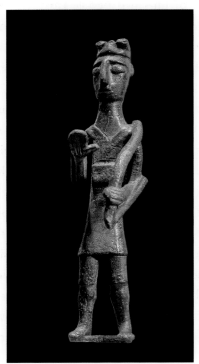

FIGURES 3.5–3.7 Small bronze figures make gestures of combat and devotion (*National Archaeological Museum of Cagliari*).

The bronzetti were valuable objects of prestige. In Sardinia, almost all were found in votive deposits, not in private tombs. They were used as gifts or for exchange, mainly with the Etruscans, and were included in rich tombs of the Etruscan aristocracy. This is another striking difference with the Mont'e Prama burials: unlike those in Italy in the same period, they did not contain any prestige objects or any apparel designed to indicate a particular social status—apart from the scaraboid, which is an isolated example that does not change the general picture.

This feature is rather uncharacteristic of any aristocracy of the time, or of any time. Professor Zucca (chapter 1) describes a society that may recall a feature of archaic Sparta—the initiation ritual that is a possible interpretation of the so-called boxers. But how far can we go with analogies in the absence of any written document? Here, we have the representation of a leading group, an aristocracy, which describes itself as a warrior society; a group that was egalitarian, not marked by differences in wealth or status, only in their functions in war. Does this self-representation refer to the actual social organization of the people or peoples who made them?

We are clueless regarding the communities that could be related to Mont'e Prama. The imposing presence of S'Urachi may be suggestive, but we have no proof of a direct relationship. Mont'e Prama is of such size and magnitude that it may be the product of different tribes that decided to build a federal heroon where the chiefs were honored. Here, we might recall analogies, like the twelve altars at Lavinium in Latium, each one marking the presence of a different people.

But we must not go too far. All these proposals are legitimate and have some elements that make us think carefully. One thing is indisputable, in my opinion: whatever its significance, and the actual value for the reconstruction of the society of the time, the people who built it had a precise design in mind—the monument must have been the product of a decision carried out over a certain number of years. In fact, the burial ground became not only a monumental cemetery, but the representation of a world that was rooted in the memory of a distant past. The numerous nuraghe models and baetyls had been removed from their site to become the guardians of the new monument, pointing to a more or less conscious revival of the past, of an ancestral civilization whose memory was still physically present, and had become objects of veneration—a proud statement of identity and prestige.

Homer comes to mind. The Homeric poems, roughly of the same period as Mont'e Prama, describe in the eighth and seventh centuries a society extant three or four hundred years earlier. The Mycenae tablets enable us to read the poems as a stratification of memory in which the contemporary society and the ancient one are inextricably linked. Homer's society is not the same as that of Mycenae and the Trojan War, but we find many features, like religion, the names of the gods, and the institutions, that continue— memories of a past that is somehow still active in a society but has undergone deep change and wants to be identified with a time that has become mythical, not unreal. With Mont'e Prama, we are not as lucky; for some reason, the late Nuragic people never adopted the Phoenician alphabet to write about themselves in their own language. So their history is lost to us, just as it was probably lost to them in any detailed sense; nonetheless, they kept memories, which we see in the bronzetti or in the nuraghe models. The people(s) who built Mont'e Prama may have mixed the real world of their time with memories of the past; in so doing they worshiped their ancestors, ennobling themselves as an elite who could refer to the imposing nuraghi and so claim power and prestige, inside and outside their community. Although it is impossible to prove this with certainty, it is the closest we can come to a plausible interpretation.

I am conscious of the fact that this essay contains more questions than answers, but this is the challenge of history—never to reach the truth, but always to aim for it, and hopefully come close to what is at least likely.

CHAPTER FOUR

Landscapes of Mont'e Prama

PETER VAN DOMMELEN, Brown University;
ALFONSO STIGLITZ, Civic Museum of San Vero Milis

T HE MOST FREQUENTLY repeated epithet used to qual-
ify both the site of Mont'e Prama and the statues of the *Giganti*
is by any measure the term "unique," with similar words like
"unparalleled" running a close second. This claim is habitually elaborated on
by pointing out that Iron Age burials are exceedingly rare in Sardinia and
that pre-Archaic life-size statuary is unheard of in most of the Mediterranean, certainly in the central and western basins and in later prehistory. Such
claims occur in popular and academic publications alike and with incessant
frequency, and they are not groundless. Their continual repetition also reen-
forces the perception that both the Mont'e Prama site and the statues are one
of a kind and can only be studied and made sense of in their own right. The
exhibitions in Sardinian museums and the dedicated website (monteprama.
it) underscore this point, even if they do offer additional materials—but dis-
cussions of relevant bronzetti and contemporary Nuragic sites are invariably
tucked away in secondary displays and deeply buried web pages.

In our contribution to this volume, we attempt to break out of this mold
not so much by foregrounding the site's contexts and the statues' parallels,
but by demonstrating how closely related and tightly integrated they were.
The fundamental significance of our proposed shift in perspective is readily
underscored by the simple fact that the people buried in the Mont'e Prama
cemetery had lived their lives elsewhere, as did those who had created and

maintained the burials and statues and who frequented the site subsequently. Our discussion is accordingly not primarily about Mont'e Prama itself but focuses on what we have termed the "landscapes" of Mont'e Prama. As we outline in what follows, we use this notion in a broad sense that goes well beyond the actual physical landscapes and settlements of the Sinis peninsula and west central Sardinia in order to achieve our goal of demonstrating that both the site and the statues of Mont'e Prama were an integral part of Iron Age Nuragic society in its later stages.

SOCIAL LANDSCAPES

Before we discuss the landscapes of the Sinis peninsula and the upper Gulf of Oristano (figure 4.1), we wish to clarify our understanding of the term "landscape" and to expand briefly on the background of this notion. As our qualification "social" already signals, we regard landscape as a concept that goes well beyond the natural or physical features of the environment, even if we do not dispute their relevance. We also explicitly look beyond the archaeological sites that attest to the settlement histories of a region, which have come to dominate the *archeologia dei paesaggi*.[1] We subscribe instead to the strand of landscape archaeology that has emerged in anglophone archaeology since the 1990s to foreground the social and cultural dimensions of landscape as a means of connecting and integrating its natural and material aspects—triangulating the notion of landscape, as it were, in social and cultural terms.[2] We accordingly consider landscape as socially constituted in the sense that "it concerns not only the physical environment *onto* which people live out their lives but also the meaningful location *in* which lives are lived."[3]

Our reasons for adopting this particular perspective are twofold. It first of all enables us to concentrate directly on the people and communities who lived in western Sardinia in the early centuries of the first millennium BCE. Second, by focusing on the people themselves, the connections between the burials at Mont'e Prama and the settlements of the region become more readily evident. In practice, our shift in perspective means that we acknowledge and start from the formal parallels and chronological connections in material culture that scholars have noted previously between Mont'e Prama and other sites and objects, such as the iconographic relations between the

Mont'e Prama statues and Iron Age bronzetti across the island or the distribution of nuraghi on the Sinis peninsula.[4] We then explore the implications and connotations of these connections to follow up on how people were situated in, moved through, and acted on the associated landscapes. In short, this approach allows us to home in on the economic, social, and cultural practices of the various communities involved and to come to an understanding of the ways in which the landscape both influenced people's lives and was in turn also shaped by human agency and identities. Rather than a mere background, landscape is from this perspective an integral feature of past (and modern) lives, and it is precisely for that reason that the social landscape approach offers a promising avenue for gaining a deeper and broader understanding of the Mont'e Prama site and late Nuragic society in west central Sardinia more generally.

In what follows, we examine three dimensions of the social landscape of the Sinis and Campidano di Milis in west central Sardinia that in our view are particularly pertinent to people's lives in the earlier centuries of the first millennium BCE. We begin with the people themselves and explore how they lived their everyday lives; we then examine the commercial and cultural contacts that Iron Age Nuragic communities maintained with Phoenicians and others beyond the Sardinian shores; and we finally turn to the abundant traces and places where the region's inhabitants connected their lives to the past and remembered their ancestors.

LANDSCAPES OF EVERYDAY LIFE

Our starting point is provided by the people from Mont'e Prama themselves, who were buried in the cemetery between the Final Bronze Age and the Iron Age. Even if Iron Age burials tend to include very few grave goods, which normally would have helped to contextualize the cemetery, the physical remains of the deceased themselves still offer important clues. The most obvious point that can be deduced is that all the individuals buried at Mont'e Prama must have lived somewhere, and it is very likely that they did so in the surrounding area. Given the topographic makeup of the Sinis, where Mont'e Prama is situated, it is most likely that the homes of these people were located somewhere on the Sinis peninsula or in the Campidano di Milis (figure 4.1). The abundance of Nuragic settlements, mostly

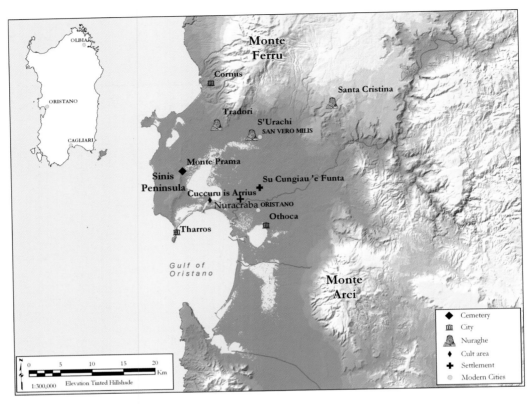

FIGURE 4.1 Map of the northern Gulf of Oristano, including the Sinis and Campidano di Milis, showing the location of Mont'e Prama and S'Urachi as well as other sites mentioned in the text (basemap by Jessica Nowlin).

single-tower nuraghi, throughout the region as attested by topographic inventories and archaeological surveys readily underscores this observation and confirms its plausibility.[5] However, a dearth of detailed evidence about the nature of these sites and the duration of their occupation makes it all but impossible to gain more specific insights.

A wealth of evidence has, by contrast, been brought to light over the past decade at the site of S'Urachi (San Vero Milis), where extensive excavations have been underway since 2013.[6] S'Urachi is a large nuraghe, situated in the Campidano di Milis, made up of multiple towers and surrounded by a massive, well-preserved external defensive wall reinforced by ten towers (figure 4.2). So far, four areas are under archaeological investigation that are all situated outside the defensive wall, as occupation of nuraghi of Iron Age

FIGURE 4.2 Aerial view of S'Urachi showing the two excavation areas, D and E, most relevant for the present discussion (van Dommelen et al. 2020; photo F. Pinna).

date and later is usually found around the monumental structure. The oldest excavated stratified contexts at S'Urachi are associated with the construction of the outer defensive wall and the stone-lined ditch right in front of it and surrounding most of the monument.[7] The wall and ditch were built together and can reliably be dated to the early seventh century BCE on the basis of both abundant ceramic evidence and absolute C14 dates.[8] A cobblestone-paved courtyard enclosed by an ashlar wall that abuts the outer defense wall can be dated to the mid- to late seventh century BCE and has provisionally been interpreted as a communal or public space. Since the last phase of Mont'e Prama, which is associated with the statues and also called the monumental phase or *necropoli Tronchetti*, tends to be dated to the eighth century BCE, the two contexts excavated at S'Urachi are evidently later, possibly as much as a century.[9]

One of the few certainties regarding the people buried at Mont'e Prama is that they represented a homogeneous and closely related group—including quite possibly in terms of kinship.[10] The physical anthropological and isotopic evidence has also been interpreted as indicative of a privileged status of the deceased, in particular those of the *tombe Tronchetti*, which of course matches very well their association with the statues. Since there are few Nuragic sites in the Sinis and the wider region around the Cabras lagoon where finds suggest regular elite residence during the Final Bronze Age to Iron Age, there are in the end only very few places where the people of Mont'e Prama plausibly may have lived. There are in fact just two nuraghi in the wider region that are surrounded by an outer defensive wall or *antemurale*, namely, S'Urachi in the Campidano di Milis and Nuracraba in the Campidano Maggiore on the northern bank of the lower Tirso.[11] The former site stands out by the length of the defensive wall (approximately 150 m, enclosing around 2,000 m²) and the inclusion of no less than ten towers—the highest number known anywhere in Sardinia. Unfortunately, very little can be said about the latter site, also known as Madonna del Rimedio, other than that it had an *antemurale* and that the site was occupied in the early Iron Age (ninth century BCE). As outlined earlier, the outer wall at S'Urachi was constructed only by the early seventh century BCE (second Iron Age).

A turreted and commanding outer defensive wall is generally regarded as projecting power and prestige, because of its relative rarity and the labor required for its construction.[12] Even if the *antemurale* at S'Urachi was most likely built after the last individual was buried at Mont'e Prama, it is equally likely that by that time the nuraghe had already become established as a prominent place in the region and the stronghold of a wealthy and well-connected family. Local wealth and especially myriad connections locally and overseas are definitely key features of the archaeological record at S'Urachi during and after the construction of the site's impressive defenses. The terrestrial meat-based diet that all deceased at Mont'e Prama had enjoyed during their lifetimes also matches the extensive faunal evidence recovered at S'Urachi from trash discarded in the ditch in later years (sixth century BCE).[13] Even if stratified early Iron Age deposits are yet to be recorded at S'Urachi, a strong indication of prestige and overseas connections is presented by a bronze torch-holder (*thymiaterion*) of East Mediterranean, likely Cypriot, origin that was found at or near S'Urachi (figure 4.3).[14] This is one of a class of rare and prestigious high-end elite items that have

FIGURE 4.3 Bronze torch-holder or *thymiaterion* found at or near S'Urachi (*National Archaeological Museum of Cagliari*).

been encountered throughout the ancient Near East and Mediterranean between the tenth and seventh centuries BCE, always and exclusively in elite contexts such as royal palaces and "princely tombs." Even if decontextualized, the object is a strong reminder that S'Urachi was already in the early Iron Age a well-connected place—precisely the kind of place that the people buried at Mont'e Prama would have hailed from.

While there is little doubt, based on current evidence, that none of the individuals buried at Mont'e Prama can be directly related to S'Urachi with any certainty, the longer-term history and the characteristics of the site over time nevertheless suggest that S'Urachi represents in all likelihood the community that the deceased from Mont'e Prama came from and were most closely associated with.

LANDSCAPES OF INTERACTION

While the significance of the Mont'e Prama statues is invariably related, if not reduced, to the absence of comparable life-size sculpture in Sardinia or elsewhere in the West Mediterranean, it is no less worth noting that the monumental phase of the *necropoli Tronchetti* with the statues signals a substantial increase of connectivity of Nuragic Iron Age communities that fits a wider pattern that has been observed across Sardinia. Nuragic Sardinia remained relatively isolated throughout the Bronze Age, as an archaeogenetic study recently underscored, even if there always was some level of overseas contact in some regions of the island.[15] The Iron Age was by contrast defined by rapidly increasing and intensifying connectivity, both in Sardinia and elsewhere.[16] From as early as the ninth century BCE, northeastern Sardinia maintained regular connections with mainland Italy, while the site of Sant'Imbenia in the Northwest became the focus of increasing connections with the (southern) Iberian Peninsula and the Phoenician world more broadly. In both cases, these contacts are attested by Nuragic finds overseas and imported materials in Nuragic contexts. By the mid-eighth century, a Phoenician settlement was first constructed on Sardinian soil at the site of Sant'Antioco (*Sulky*) on the southern tip of Sardinia.[17]

In west central Sardinia, comparable, though subtly different, overseas contacts are signaled by the life-size and stone sculpted statues of the monumental phase at Mont'e Prama. Even if the iconographic details of the statues are clearly and consistently based on the so-called bronzetti figurines, and while stoneworking was a well-established Nuragic craft, the idea of life-size, free-standing statuary was new to Nuragic Sardinia, and its appearance at Mont'e Prama may therefore be understood in the context of overseas contacts, which possibly reached as far afield as the northern Levantine coast.[18] A much more specific pointer is the scarab sealstone found in burial 25 at Mont'e Prama that similarly refers to the eastern Mediterranean, in particular the shores of the southern Levant.[19] Elsewhere in the region, the previously mentioned torch-holder from S'Urachi seamlessly fits in the same category of elite connections with the eastern Mediterranean, while locally produced Phoenician-style amphorae of the Sant'Imbenia type at Nuraxinieddu and Su Padrigheddu, situated near S'Urachi, offer further testimony to regular interactions with the Phoenician world of the western Mediterranean throughout the eighth and seventh centuries BCE.[20] While these amphorae offer the earliest and most evident examples of hybrid manufacturing practices, the evidence from S'Urachi and Su Padrigheddu demonstrates that overseas innovations were also increasingly used to produce multiple other vessel shapes and types, including cooking pots.[21] The stone-lined ditch that was constructed at S'Urachi in the early seventh century BCE as part of the defenses surrounding the nuraghe offers yet another instance of overseas contacts, as defensive ditches were unknown in Nuragic Sardinia but were, on the contrary, a well-attested feature of Iron Age Phoenician architecture and became a regular appearance in Iberian settlements from the eighth century onward.[22] The San Marco peninsula, finally, where the Phoenician settlement of *Tharros* was established by the end of the seventh century, is also likely to have been a key place in these interactions, but there is at present insufficient evidence for the Nuragic site of Su Muru Mannu to understand its nature in the Iron Age—even if the later presence of Phoenician settlers and its proximity to Mont'e Prama strongly suggest some level and form of interaction.[23]

What unites most of these instances of overseas connectivity and what in our view defines the landscape of interaction in west central Sardinia is that local Iron Age communities, or at least sections of them, were actively involved in these contacts. We can point to both local artisans and local elites as having played an active role in the production and consumption of the material culture listed earlier: Nuragic stonemasons crafted the Mont'e Prama statues and, somewhat later, constructed the stone embankments of the defensive ditch at S'Urachi, while throughout this period Nuragic potters drew on local ceramic traditions to manufacture a new type of transport vessels. In all these cases, they were inspired by or worked to specifications directly or indirectly provided from overseas.[24] At the same time, this landscape of interaction is also intimately and irrevocably associated with local elites, who may be assumed to have played a key part in both commissioning and using the products of these hybrid artisanal practices. A consistent and in our view defining feature of these landscapes is therefore the active role played by Nuragic communities in overseas interactions and the enduring prominence of Nuragic traditions over the centuries of the Iron Age.

The latter point is well captured by the detailed evidence on ceramic production from S'Urachi and Su Padrigheddu, which shows how this process started in the later eighth century BCE and may be traced in successive transformations over the following centuries. By the sixth century BCE, it resulted in the production of typologically Phoenician vessels with multiple technical characteristics that were rooted in Nuragic manufacturing traditions.[25] The life-size statues and imported sealstone at Mont'e Prama thus fit comfortably within this enduring and evolving landscape of interactions.

LANDSCAPES OF MEMORY

The Mont'e Prama statues are not isolated at the site itself either. In addition to the life-size human representations, there are multiple dozens of stone sculptures of nuraghi, some of which reach up to half a meter in height. These are evidently far from life-size and may in fact best be defined as miniatures. There are also at least fifteen standing stones that are of regular size, which is around one meter tall. All the former and most of the latter are made from the same soft sandstone as the statues, which is local to the Sinis.[26]

Nuraghe "models" or miniatures are a well-established category of Nuragic material culture that is found throughout Sardinia and represents a key characteristic of the Iron Age. They exist in stone and in bronze, with the latter usually substantially smaller than the former. While the larger ones, whether in stone or bronze, tend to be quite detailed, the smaller ones are, on the whole, rather stylized. The smallest may have been mounted on a stone pedestal or even a portable pole, much like regular bronzetti.[27] Even if many of these miniatures are without a recorded context, there is a sufficient percentage properly documented to confirm that they are consistently associated with ritual and elite contexts. That is admittedly still a broad categorization, but even the limited documentation points to the so-called meeting huts as a preferred place for stone miniatures. The few properly documented cases, such as at Su Nuraxi (Barumini) and Palmavera (Alghero), also make it clear that these miniature nuraghi took pride of place by being positioned on a pedestal in the center of the circular room, surrounded by the bench against the wall where elites would have been seated. Other miniatures, especially those in bronze, have been found at sanctuaries, in particular the large "federal" ones.

The common denominator of these contexts is that of display and the projection of power.[28] There is yet more to these objects, because miniature nuraghi have primarily been recorded at sites such as the large sanctuaries and "meeting huts" that had come to prominence as Nuragic society underwent major transformations over the centuries around the turn of the millennium. In the course of this process, "real nuraghi" were no longer built anew, and social and political life shifted to villages—at least in the largest nuraghe complexes that may be most readily associated with elites.[29] It is at the same time no less significant that as large multiroom houses organized around a courtyard became the focal point of everyday life, all these new villages remained physically close to a preexisting nuraghe—there is no evidence of settlements of courtyard houses founded entirely *ex novo*.[30] The importance of nuraghi was thus transferred to the miniatures that symbolically bestowed the monuments' and the occupants' power and prestige to the new centers of political life. It is clearly no coincidence that as multiroom courtyard houses became the norm for daily life, these meeting huts reproduced the Bronze Age roundhouses that had been abandoned in daily life. In other words, Nuragic Iron Age society, at least in its elite and ritual spheres, evoked the past in general and the nuraghe in particular as emblems of community and power, as they literally rallied around the miniature reproductions that "epitomize, echo and reverberate meanings."[31]

The dozens of miniature nuraghi at Mont'e Prama are an unusually high concentration, but they are not the only ones in the Sinis, where eight more such miniatures have been found.[32] Two of these, moreover, are highly unusual, as they include human and animal figurines and thus seem to tell a story that evidently involved a nuraghe (figure 4.4). While no meeting hut has yet come to light in the Sinis or Campidano di Milis, including at S'Urachi, it is worth noting that a monumental circular building of late Nuragic date has been excavated at Mont'e Prama, on the western side of the road, away from the burials. The absence of a bench against the wall does not support identification as a regular meeting hut, but even so the reference to the circular roundhouses is evident.[33]

FIGURE 4.4 A miniature nuraghe from the site called Serra is Araus, with the representation of a person and an animal (*Civic Museum of San Vero Milis*).

The standing stones at Mont'e Prama also fit neatly in this picture, albeit in a different way, because they reference monoliths that were regular features of Bronze Age communal "Giants' Tombs." These tombs were used for burial of selected individuals throughout the Nuragic period and are defined by an impressive megalithic façade that in many instances included one or more rows of standing stones. It is therefore entirely appropriate that fifteen of such standing stones were part of the display at Mont'e Prama, some of which were probably sculpted anew, while others may well have been recovered from older "Giants' Tombs."[34]

Taken together, there is solid evidence that the Sinis and Campidano di Milis also constituted a well-established and elaborate landscape of memory that integrated the display and activities at Mont'e Prama intimately and actively with the surrounding region.

CONTEXTUALIZING MONT'E PRAMA

The evidence outlined in this brief essay clearly suggests, we contend in conclusion, that the Sinis and Campidano di Milis represent key contexts for understanding the site of Mont'e Prama, with its remarkable burials and statuary. The notion of landscape has helped us to bring together aspects of people's and communities' lives that are usually considered separately. The element of memory, or more generally "engagement with the past," is particularly significant in our view, not only because it has long been recognized as a defining characteristic of the Iron Age, but also, and perhaps even more so, because a true landscape of memory can be traced in the Sinis and Campidano di Milis that is closely intertwined with people's everyday lives in the Nuragic Iron Age.

While we certainly do not wish to diminish the importance of Mont'e Prama or to downplay the multiple unusual features of the site, we hope to have shown that Mont'e Prama was a remarkable and meaningful place in Iron Age west central Sardinia and that its significance largely derived from its deep roots in the local landscapes of the northern Gulf of Oristano. The multiple overlapping landscapes that all include Mont'e Prama also underscore that the site is not only or even primarily a cemetery, even if burying people was a key feature of it. It was most of all a meaningful and prominent place in these landscapes and, by implication, in people's daily lives.

The site of S'Urachi features prominently in our discussion of the landscapes of Mont'e Prama, which may in part be ascribed to our sustained and careful research at the site that has brought to light extensive and detailed evidence of the local community and its elite, their perceptions and interests, and strong local roots. It also underscores that S'Urachi and Mont'e Prama are the few, if not the only, sites in the region that were consistently part of the social landscapes we examined. The evidence from S'Urachi consistently matches that of Mont'e Prama, albeit in various ways and despite the obvious differences between a habitation site and burial ground. In structural terms, we submit, the two sites may indeed be regarded as complementary and closely matching.

NOTES

1. See, for example, E. Garau, *Disegnare paesaggi della Sardegna* (Ortacesus: Nuove Grafiche Puddu, 2007); F. Cambi, *Manuale di archeologia dei paesaggi: metodologie, fonti, contesti*, Manuali universitari 106 (Rome: Carocci, 2011).

2. W. Ashmore, "Social Archaeologies of Landscape," in *A Companion to Social Archaeology*, ed. L. Meskell and R. Preucel (Malden, Mass.: Blackwell 2004), 259–61; cf. W. Ashmore and A. B. Knapp, eds., *Archaeologies of Landscape: Contemporary Perspectives* (Malden, Mass.: Blackwell 1999).

3. B. David and J. Thomas, "Landscape Archaeology: Introduction," in *Handbook of Landscape Archaeology*, ed. David and Thomas, World Archaeological Congress Research Handbooks in Archaeology (Walnut Creek, Calif.: Leftcoast Press 2008), 38; cf. Ashmore, "Social Archaeologies of Landscape."

4. For example, F. Lo Schiavo, "La scultura nuragica, dai bronzi figurati alle statue di Mont'e Prama," in *Le sculture di Mont'e Prama. La mostra*, ed. A. Usai (Rome: Gangemi, 2014), 99–110; A. Usai, "Paesaggi nuragici," in *L'isola delle torri. Giovanni Lilliu e la Sardegna nuragica*, ed. M. Minoja, G. F. Salis, and L. Usai (Sassari: Carlo Delfino, 2015), 58–69.

5. A. Usai, "Paesaggi nuragici"; P. G. Spanu and B. Panico, "Archeologia dei paesaggi di Mont'e Prama," in *I riti della morte e del culto di Mont'e Prama—Cabras*, ed. M. Torelli, Atti dei Convegni dei Lincei 303 (Rome: Bardi Edizioni, 2016), 31–47; P. G. Spanu and B. Panico, "Archeologia dei paesaggi di Mont'e Prama," in *I riti della morte e del culto di Mont'e Prama—Cabras*, ed. M. Torelli, Atti dei Convegni dei Lincei 303 (Rome: Bardi Edizioni, 2016), 31–47; A. Stiglitz, "Mobilità dei paesaggi tharrensi. L'Età del Ferro nell'aread el Golfo di Oristano (Sardegna)," *Cuadernos de Prehistoria de la Universidad de Granada* 31 (2021): 211–31.

6. P. van Dommelen et al., "Progetto S'Urachi: incontri culturali intorno a un nuraghe di età fenicio-punica," in *Un viaje entre el Oriente y el Occidente del Mediterráneo. Actas del IX Congreso Internacional de Estudios Fenicios y Púnicos*, ed. S. Celestino Pérez and E. Rodríguez González, MYTRA 5 (Mérida: CSIC et al., 2020), 1627–36. The Progetto S'Urachi started in 2013, directed by the present coauthors and with the support of the Museo Civico of San Vero Milis and the Joukowsky Institute of Brown University, and continues to this day. Formal permission for fieldwork has been granted and confirmed every three years by the Italian Ministry of Culture to the Comune of San Vero Milis, at the generous intercession of the Soprintendenza archeologica in Cagliari. For detailed information, including annual reports and (mostly open access) publications, see http://blogs.brown.edu/surachi. A full publication of the excavation of the antemurale and ditch (Area E) is forthcoming and in many instances will provide more detailed information than the published preliminary reports referenced in the text.

7. R. Deiana et al., "FDEM and ERT Measurements for Archaeological Prospections at Nuraghe S'Urachi (West-Central Sardinia)," *Archaeological Prospection* 28: FirstView (2021), https://doi.org/10.1002/arp.838.

8. P. van Dommelen et al., "Un millennio di storie: nuove notizie preliminari sul progetto S'Urachi (San Vero Milis, OR), 2016–2018," *Quaderni della Soprintendenza Archeologia, Belle Arti e Paesaggio per la città metropolitana di Cagliari e le province di Oristano e Sud Sardegna* 29 (2018): 147–48, https://quaderniarcheocaor.beniculturali.it.

9. L. Lai et al., "Isotopi stabili e radioattivi: primi dati su dieta e cronologia assoluta delle sepolture di Mont'e Prama," in *Le sculture di Mont'e Prama. Contesto, scavi e materiali*, ed. M. Minoja and A. Usai (Rome: Gangemi, 2014), 214–16; A. Usai, "Mont'e Prama 2015. Nota preliminare," *Quaderni della Soprintendenza Archeologica per le province di Cagliari e Oristano* 26 (2015): 87–89, https://quaderniarcheocaor.beniculturali.it.

10. R. Cameriere et al., "L'età dei defunti di Mont'e Prama: un aspetto interessante e cruciale," in Minoja and Usai, *Le sculture di Mont'e Prama*, 201–6; O. Fonzo and E. Pacciani, "Gli inumati nella necropoli di Mont'e Prama," in Minoja and Usai, *Le sculture di Mont'e Prama*, 184; Lai et al., "Isotopi stabili e radioattivi," 214.

11. Stiglitz, "Mobilità dei paesaggi tharrensi"; A. Vanzetti et al., "Complessi fortificati della Sardegna e delle isole del Mediterraneo occidentale nella protostoria," *Scienze dell'Antichità* 19, nos. 2–3 (2013): 110–13.

12. Vanzetti et al. "Complessi fortificati della Sardegna e delle isole del Mediterraneo occidentale nella protostoria," 90–92; G. Webster, *The Archaeology of Nuragic Sardinia*, Monographs in Mediterranean Archaeology 14 (Sheffield, UK: Equinox 2015), 109–10.

13. G. Pérez Jordà et al., "Iron Age Botanical Remains from Nuraghe S'Urachi (Sardinia, Italy)," *Antiquity* 94 (2020): 374, https://doi.org/10.15184/aqy.2020.33; D. Ramis et al., "Aproximación a la explotación de los recursos faunísticos en el poblado de S'Urachi (Cerdeña) en época fenicia," in *La alimentación en el mundo púnico: producciones, procesos y*

consumos, ed. C. Gómez Bellard, G. Pérez Jordà, and A. Vendrell, BetíSPAL Monografías Arqueología 32 (Seville: Universidad de Sevilla, 2020), 113–28.

14. A. Stiglitz, "Dal torciere al workshop. L'età del Ferro a San Vero Milis," *Rivista di Studi Fenici* 41 (2014): 16–17.

15. J. Marcus et al., "Genetic History from the Middle Neolithic to Present on the Mediterranean Island of Sardinia," *Nature Communications* 11, no. 939 (November 2020), https://doi.org/10.1038/s41467-020-14523-6; A. B. Knapp, A. Russell, and P. van Dommelen, "Cyprus, Sardinia and Sicily: A Maritime Perspective on Interaction, Connectivity and Imagination in Mediterranean Prehistory," *Cambridge Archaeological Journal* 31 (2022): 79–97.

16. P. van Dommelen and A. Roppa, "Conclusioni: per una definizione dell'età del Ferro sarda," *Rivista di Studi Fenici* 41 (2014): 271–77.

17. E. Pompianu and A. Unali, "Le origini della colonizzazione fenicia in Sardegna: Sulky," in *Contextualising Early Colonisation: Archaeology, Sources, Chronology and Interpretative Models between Italy and the Mediterranean*, ed. L. Donnellan, V. Nizzo, and G. J. Burgers, Forum Romanum Belgicum 13 (Rome: Belgisch Historisch Instituut te Rome, 2016), 13.12; I. Oggiano and T. Pedrazzi, "Contacts et interactions entre 'Phéniciens' et Sardes au début du 1er millénaire av. J.C.: le cas des amphores vinaires," in *Les Phéniciens, les Puniques et les autres. Echanges et identités en Méditerranée ancienne*, ed. L. Bonadies, I. Chirpanlieva, and E. Guillon, Orient & Méditerranée 31 (Paris: Editions de Boccard 2019), 223–57; S. Amicone et al., "New Insights Into Early Iron Age Connections Between Sardinia and Etruria: Archaeometric Analyses of Ceramics from Tavolara," *Journal of Archaeological Science: Reports* 33 (2020): 102452.

18. M. Rendeli, "Monte 'e Prama: 4875 punti interrogativi," in *Meetings Between Cultures in the Ancient Mediterranean. Proceedings of the 17th International Congress of Classical Archaeology, Rome 22–26 Sept. 2008*, ed. M. Dalla Riva and H. Di Giuseppe, Bollettino di Archeologia Online 0, volume speciale (Rome: Ministero per I Beni e le Attività Culturali, D-2-7, 2010), https://bollettinodiarcheologiaonline.beniculturali.it/; I. van Kampen, "La statuaria e il rapporto con l'ambiente Nord Siriano," in *Meetings Between Cultures in the Ancient Mediterranean*, F-7-4.

19. A. Stiglitz, "Lo scaraboide della tomba 25," in Minoja and Usai, *Le sculture di Mont'e Prama*, 323–30.

20. Oggiano and Pedrazzi, "Contacts et interactions entre 'Phéniciens' et Sardes," 238–43.

21. A. Roppa, "Colonial Encounters and Artisanal Practices in the Western Phoenician World: Ceramic Evidence from Sardinia," *Rivista di Studi Fenici* 47 (2019): 59–61.

22. A. Lorrio, "Fosos en los sistemas defensivos del Levante ibérico (siglos VIII–II a.C.)," *Revista d'Arqueologia de Ponent* 22 (2012): 59–86.

23. Stiglitz, "Mobilità dei paesaggi tharrensi," 221.

24. Roppa, "Colonial Encounters and Artisanal Practices," 61–63.

25. Roppa, "Colonial Encounters and Artisanal Practices"; A. Roppa and E. Madrigali, "Colonial Production and Urbanization in Iron Age to Early Punic Sardinia (8th–5th c. BC)," in *Making Cities: Economies of Production and Urbanization in Mediterranean Europe 1000–500 BC*, ed. M. Gleba, B. Marín-Aguilera, and B. Dimova (Cambridge: McDonald Institute, 2021), 299–312.

26. V. Leonelli, "I modelli di nuraghe e altri elementi scultorei di Mont'e Prama," in Minoja and Usai, *Le sculture di Mont'e Prama*, 263–92; E. Usai, "Idoli betilici di Mont'e Prama," in Minoja and Usai, *Le sculture di Mont'e Prama*, 293–314; A. Stiglitz, "La memoria dei nuraghi. Raffigurazioni turrite nell'entroterra tharrense (Sardegna centro-occidentale)," *Quaderni della Soprintendenza Archeologia, Belle Arti e Paesaggio per la città metropolitana di Cagliari e le province di Oristano e Sud Sardegna* 32, no. 1 (2021): 116, https://www.quaderniarcheocaor.beniculturali.it/index.php/qua/article/view/49/58.

27. E. Blake, "Strategic Symbolism: Miniature Nuraghi of Sardinia," *Journal of Mediterranean Archaeology* 10, 2 (1997): 151–64; F. Campus and V. Leonelli, *La Sardegna nuragica. Miti e simboli di una civiltà mediterranea* (Monteriggioni: ARA edizioni, 2014).

28. C. Tronchetti, "Il segno del potere," in *Papers of the Fourth Conference of Italian Archaeology. The Archaeology of Power 2*, ed. E. Herring, R. Whitehouse, and J. Wilkins (London: Accordia Research Institute 1991), 207–19.

29. Vanzetti et al., "Complessi fortificati della Sardegna e delle isole del Mediterraneo," 96–97; C. Tronchetti, "Cultural Interactions in Iron Age Sardinia," in *The Cambridge Prehistory of the Bronze & Iron Age Mediterranean*, ed. A. B. Knapp and P. van Dommelen (New York: Cambridge University Press, 2014), 266–84.

30. Webster, *The Archaeology of Nuragic Sardinia*, 155–57.

31. L. Foxhall, "Introduction: Miniaturization," *World Archaeology* 47, 1 (2015): 1.

32. Stiglitz, "Mobilità dei paesaggi tharrensi," 113–17. It is practically impossible to give precise numbers of the miniature nuraghi found, in part because numbers of fragments have been confused with the minimum number of individuals (MNI), and in part because find contexts have been poorly recorded, if they are known at all. The question of MNI affects the numbers cited for Mont'e Prama in particular. To add to the confusion, the miniature nuraghe from Cann'e Vadosu could effectively be added to those of Mont'e Prama, as it was found just beyond the current archaeological site. For a detailed discussion, see Stiglitz, "Mobilità dei paesaggi tharrensi"; C. Nocco, "Modelli di nuraghe," in *Mont'e Prama-I. Ricerche 2014*, ed. G. Ranieri and R. Zucca (Cagliari: Carlo Delfino, 2015), 254–64.

33. A. Usai, "Mont'e Prama 2015. Nota preliminare," 86–87.

34. E. Usai, "Idoli betilici di Mont'e Prama."

CHAPTER FIVE

The Restoration and Conservation
of the Giants of Mont'e Prama

ROBERTO NARDI, Archaeological Conservation
Center of Rome

T he multimillennium history of the sculptures of Mont'e Prama
is characterized by events that are partly only hypothetical, starting from the origin of the sculptures and their circumstances to
their original location, their relationship with the tombs of young warriors
near which the fragments were found, their destruction into ten thousand
fragments, and finally the circumstances that allowed their discovery. The
history lasts almost thirty centuries, until that day in 1974 when Sisinnio
Podda, a farmer from Cabras, accidentally brought to light the first finds and
communicated their existence to the authorities: that episode marked the
beginning of the modern history of the sculptures of Mont'e Prama with
the archaeological excavation of 1975–1979.[1] The history culminates in the
cultural restoration and conservation project, the salient phases of which I
will describe in this essay.

An important premise of this story is the recognition of the titanic
work of the "approach and construction" of the project, carried out by Dr.
Antonietta Boninu, archaeologist of the Soprintendenza per i Beni Archeologici di Sassari, in the 1990s.[2] Nothing would have been possible without
the network she wove with great wisdom and kindness, which was able to
generate the political conditions necessary to create the beneficial (and rare)
synergy between the Ministero dei Beni Culturali, the Regione Sardegna,
and the Soprintendenza.

These institutions have all been focused on a common goal: to financially, logistically, and technically enable a cultural project whose objective was the rebirth of the sculptures, to make them usable in a single location, and to make them known to the world. This synergy made available the necessary funds for the project, as well as the establishment of a center for restoration and conservation at Li Punti (in Sassari), which was essential for carrying out a conservation intervention as ambitious as it is complex. This intervention began with a long preliminary study undertaken by the officials of the Soprintendenza per i Beni Archeologici di Sassari to develop the guidelines for the competition—the "concorso"—that would select the conservators (figure 5.1).

Stimulated by the originality of the competition launched by the Regione Sardegna and the Superintendency, which was not based exclusively on the principle of accepting the least expensive offer but also weighed

FIGURE 5.1 Antonietta Boninu talks with conservators at the Li Punti Center about the alignment of an archer statue on its support structure.

technical and cultural aspects, the Centro di Conservazione Archeologica di Roma (CCA; Archaeological Conservation Center) made a proposal.[3] The CCA is a private company of conservators who graduated from the Istituto Centrale di Roma and have worked on public commissions in the field of cultural heritage conservation since 1982, with projects such as the restoration of the arch of Septimius Severus in the Roman Forum, the statuary collection of the Capitoline Museum in Rome, and the restoration of the Tomba del Capo in the necropolis of Sant'Andrea Priu in Bonorva, Sardinia. Keenly aware of the extraordinary and universal importance of the archaeological discovery of Mont'e Prama, the CCA invested all its skills to generate a cultural project up to the potential of the new Mont'e Prama phenomenon—a cultural project whose very title, "Mont'e Prama—Prenda 'e Zenia," declared its intention to reconstitute the direct line between the sculptures and the culture of Sardinia (as "Prenda 'e Zenia" means "Jewel of the Lineage").

We have not seen the minutes of the meeting of the committee that judged the submitted proposals, but from comments collected informally in the following years, we can say that the CCA's proposal was considered complete, with a broad spectrum of action, strong cultural content, and economic feasibility. This last point—economic feasibility—became even clearer to the administration as the work progressed, given that the contractual goal was to set up a pair of sculptures, while the CCA returned forty-four of them (despite considering only those with a defined "personality").[4] The achievement is even more impressive if we take into account how much more the conservators, with the experience they gained, would be able to assemble by including the new findings that emerged during the excavation campaigns carried out after the restoration.

THE CULTURAL PROGRAM

Exactly 5,178 bio-limestone fragments, weighing a total of 9,140 kg, were transferred from the Cagliari deposits to the new premises of the Li Punti Center and exhibited there by officials of the Superintendency of Sassari. The individual fragments varied in weight from a few hundred grams up to torso portions that exceeded 100 kilos. Together they created an endless array of anatomical parts mixed with shapeless and anonymous pieces that at first glance appeared like an immense puzzle without any reference image (figure 5.2).

When the intervention began, the iconography that the fragments would assume once they were reassembled was only hypothesized. The feeling such an expanse of stone fragments conveyed to those who saw for the first time the rows of tables with multiple anatomical elements classified by category was variable and subjective: from amazement to disbelief, from discouragement to curiosity, from wonder to appreciation. In technicians accustomed to such interventions, the first feeling was one of enthusiasm and optimism, in the certainty that the result would come. With patience, perseverance, trust, and good organization, the sculptures would take shape again. And so they did.

Before processing the fragments, some preliminary operations were necessary: the fragments were photographed, studied, assigned an inventory

FIGURE 5.2 Tables full of anatomical parts and other fragments (laid out in preparation for executive planning of the restoration) in one of many rooms in the Li Punti Center equipped by Antonietta Boninu, Gonaria Demontis, and Alba Canu of Sardinia's Superintendency for Archaeological Heritage.

number, documented, registered, and entered in a database. Subsequently, vulnerable fragments were detected and treated with appropriate methods and techniques. The analysis of the degradation mechanisms and of the alterations of the material, in addition to the study of the original pieces and ancient execution techniques, is an essential element of any conservation and restoration intervention.

The information collected during the excavation provided little data helpful for dealing with the complexity of such a gigantic puzzle. Thus the careful and close observation of the individual fragments and the classification of every slight clue were the essential tools in identifying relationships between the finds. At the same time, further diagnostic investigations were performed to supplement those envisaged in the preliminary plan and implemented prior to the executive phase. These chemical, physical, and petrographic investigations were carried out on the original material, on both the natural and the artificial surface deposits, and on the forms of deterioration, with the aim of identifying the functional characteristics of the materials, to define the intervention in detail, and to further analyze some details identified during the documentation and cleaning phases. Documentation continuously preceded and followed intervention. The survey and graphic documentation, the photography and videos, and the diagnostic analyses have absorbed 10 percent of the resources of the entire project. The quantity of data to be recorded made it clear from the initial stage that, considering the number of fragments, it was essential to proceed with the creation of a digital archive, which would allow for easy management of all the information collected. For this purpose, a database with a flexible and modifiable structure was created, which would respond to the fundamental need of the intervention: namely, to provide useful data for the search for connections between the fragments during the reassembly and assembly of the sculptures (figure 5.3).

Once the state of the surfaces was documented and the degradation mechanisms understood, we proceeded with the treatment of the stone. Following a "soft" methodology, the interventions were limited, and each technical operation was performed with respect for the material, the original finishes, the patinas of time, and the marks of history. The result is the collection of the sculptures of Mont'e Prama as seen today: a myriad of

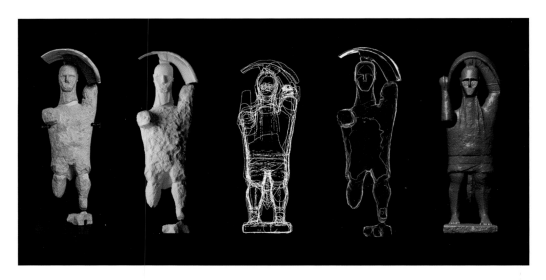

FIGURE 5.3 An example of the documentation process, from photographic relief to three-dimensional scanning to the digital restitution of the original shapes.

stone fragments restored—not transformed, but simply returned—to their original arrangement. The cleaning was carried out through progressive phases, starting with the most delicate operations with a milder effect, to increasingly efficient interventions in relation to the type of deposit to be removed (figures 5.4 and 5.5).

Through various initial tests, the most suitable system for the sculptures was selected: atomized water, one of the milder and less invasive cleaning techniques, developed by the CCA in the 1980s during the restoration of the arch of Septimius Severus in the Roman Forum. Vaporized at low pressure (the water:air ratio can reach the value of 1:400, operating at a pressure of 1.2 PSI), the water is able to soften the surface deposits. These are then reduced and removed with scalpels, spiral drills, and micro drills.

Once the cleaning was complete, we moved on to consolidation. Starting from the methodological principle of respect for the original material, consolidation was limited to necessary cases: fragments that did not show defects in surface cohesion did not receive consolidating treatments. For the others, however, the operation was performed with inorganic materials— lime water and ethyl silicate—applied by brush or immersion.

FIGURE 5.4 The limited restoration operations were carried out with respect for the material, original finishes, patinas of time, and marks of history.

FIGURE 5.5 Conservators engaged in the restoration work for more than five thousand working days.

The next step, the gluing of contiguous fragments, was performed using a two-component epoxy resin paste, Etobond, applied to a reversible film of Paraloid B72 at 15 percent acetone. In general, all the discontinuities of the material, such as cracks and contact lines in the fragments, were grouted with a lime-based mortar, compatible with the original material in terms of color and chemical structure. In the case of fragments that were not contiguous but pertinent to each other, gluing was not carried out: the find was left detached from the rest of the sculpture, positioned in the attributed location by means of independent arms fixed to the metal support.

Reassembling the fragments without using pins and without making holes was an imperative for the whole project, based as it was on the principle of maximum respect for the original material. This criterion was applied rigidly, and the sculptures were re-erected thanks to the metal structure of the support—the result of effective collaboration among archaeologists, conservators, engineers, and iron crafters.

The extreme fragility of the recomposed sculptures and the complexity of the ensembles to be exhibited—consisting of consolidated stone finds, glued with the aid of epoxy resins without internal pins, with pertinent but not contiguous elements simply positioned close to each other—have made it even more complicated to develop articulated and specialized supports and have required creative solutions on an ad hoc basis (all this without relinquishing formal unity and the criteria of stability, reversibility, and the ease of disassembly and reassembly, which are the basis of the project).

The reassembled sculptures immediately posed a series of very specific technical challenges in defining the design of the exhibition supports, which we can summarize as follows: the two categories of sculptures—statues and nuraghe models—had to be mounted on a vertical support, to a height corresponding to the original position with respect to the base; the support had to allow a stereometric vision of the sculpture, interfering as little as possible with the visual perception of the whole, both on the physical level (impeded vision) and on the aesthetic level (altered/conditioned vision on the formal level); the support had to ensure the absolute stability of the sculpture and ease of handling inside the museum, taking weight and size into account, and the need to lift it with simple means, such as a transpallet; the support and fixing points had to act through gravity and contrast, effectively holding the sculpture for the purposes of both exhibition and possible internal movement within the museum, without damaging the integrity of the stone material, taking into account both its vulnerability to breakage and its sensitivity to surface abrasion; no pins could be inserted into the original material; and finally, the whole fixing system had to be reversible, be easy to assemble and disassemble, permit additions from further archaeological finds to complete the reconstruction of the sculpture, and, above all, be inobtrusive from an aesthetic point of view. All anchoring systems had to be reversible, while still guaranteeing the stability of the sculptures positioned on the support, and at no point could the metal elements come into direct contact with the original stone material—the contact points had to be mediated by synthetic insulating interfaces.

In compliance with these objectives, the sculptures' support structure was designed to meet the following requirements: categorical exclusion of the insertion of metal pins after drilling the stone material; minimal deformability of the whole, in order to decrease the risk of accidental breakage of stone parts as a result of structural movements, small impacts, oscillations, thermal ranges, etc.; minimal visibility of the metal structure, both for the vertical supports and for the horizontal extensions supporting protruding parts; maximal stability of the support, also in consideration of small impacts compatible with a museum environment; safe connection between contact points and stone, to avoid damage due to crushing and/or abrasion; feasibility of making successive additions of corresponding and pertinent fragments; and maximal suitability of the structure for exhibition in a museum environment.

The accommodation of all these requirements went through progressive revisions, reinterpretations, and remodulations until the design solution was eventually adopted. The system was set up on linear supports, so as to resolve in a simple and harmonious way the dichotomy between the first two essential requirements: minimizing the structure's visibility and at the same time minimizing its deformability. For this purpose, we chose materials with high resistance, low technology, and minimal dimensions. The designed shape is a framework consisting of a central column placed behind the back of the statue with arms that extend from the column to the back and sides to support the protruding parts (figure 5.6).

The dimensioning of the framework was carried out on the basis of a load analysis that was as faithful as possible to reality, while also trying to translate

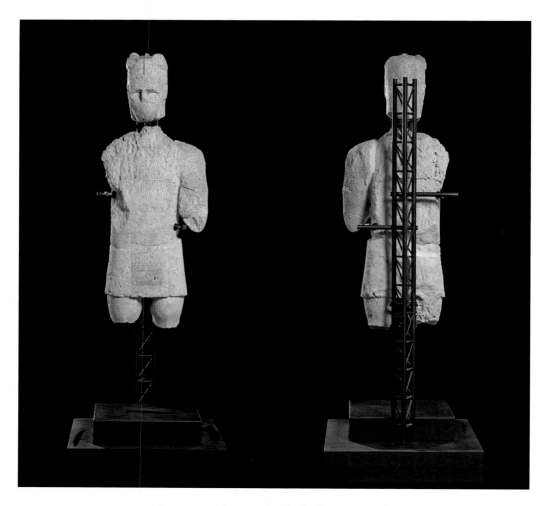

FIGURE 5.6 It was crucial to reassemble the fragments without using pins and without making holes in the stone. The metal support structure was the result of collaboration among archaeologists, conservators, engineers, and iron craftsmen.

into numerical terms accidental events—small impacts compatible with a museum environment—and maintaining large security margins, both for the static load (that is, the total weight of the sculptures) and for accidents such as small bumps during handling or direct contact with the public.

The support of the statue is entrusted entirely to a bracket placed under the subject's crotch in the sculptures of archers and warriors (figures 5.7 and 5.8), and one bracket (or more) arranged under or on the sides of the

FIGURE 5.7 The support structure is a framework that has a central column behind the statue, with a main bracket and secondary arms.

FIGURE 5.8 In many cases, a sculpture is supported by one bracket beneath the subject's crotch; in other cases, one or more brackets are arranged under or alongside the subject's legs. The arms of the structure serve only to maintain the sculpture in position.

legs in the case of the boxers, when the perizoma or parts of it are present. The secondary arms of the structure are therefore entrusted only with the functions of fixing and maintaining the sculpture in position.

Where the shape of the sculpture allowed the insertion of metal elements inside the fractures, threaded aluminum cylinders (*boccole*) were used, fixed inside the epoxy resin shims without intervening on the original material. The *boccole* are integrated with the framework by using short, simple metal arms with a rectangular section. The base of the framework consists of a plate of sufficient weight and width to ensure the stability of the whole and allow a standard hold for handling. Three types of fastening have been provided, all reversible, to ease removal of the sculpture: resting, contrasting, and threaded *boccole*.

The support fixings are those typical of brackets, in which the weight and friction ensure the stability of the contact. The antishock material mediated the functions of load distribution and protection of the stone material. They were arranged in pairs on the sides of the trunk, in a position as hidden by the limbs as possible. The arms' function was completed with the use of screw clamps whose heads were fitted with ball joints made of antishock material.

The contact elements are in plastic material (thermoplastic elastomers), either simply interposed between the stone and the steel or inserted in special cone bases with a ball joint, made of PA6 (polyamide technopolymer) and reinforced with graphite and 30 percent fiberglass, which is particularly resistant to wear, abrasion, and compression (it is a material that is suitable for the production of mechanical fittings of various sizes, even in critical environments) (figures 5.9 and 5.10).

For the finish of the support structure, including brackets and arms, a dark color (micaceous anthracite black) was chosen, made with powder paints and the addition of metallic pigments. This kind of finish, deliberately coarse and neutral, neither ancient nor modern, provisional in character, perfectly combines with the material aspect of the limestone and the ongoing nature of the recomposition. At the same time, the dark color lends itself well to exhibition on a dark backdrop: the support is absorbed by the backdrop, allowing the sculpture to stand out in all its visual impact (figure 5.11).

The work on the support design also included a series of additional, transport-related elements, which are not visible in the exhibition. Each

FIGURE 5.9 The sculptures' support structure has been designed to allow subsequent additions of pertinent fragments.

FIGURE 5.10 Reversible anchoring systems guarantee the stability of the sculptures on the support. At no point are metal elements in direct contact with the original stone material: all are mediated by synthetic insulating interfaces.

FIGURE 5.11 The black metal finish allows the support structure to disappear against the dark backdrop so the sculpture can stand out.

sculpture has its own technical kit, designed to park it in an antishock safety position, without removing it from the support. CCA technicians extensively tested these kits during transport from the Li Punti Center to Cabras and Cagliari, demonstrating their efficiency—they allowed a transfer to the upper floors of the museum in absolute safety.

The sculptures are meant to be exhibited in a museum setting, not outdoors. For this reason, no protective products were applied in the final treatment of the surfaces. All the sculptures have been left in natural stone to avoid contamination with products unrelated to the original material, which can never be sufficiently stable. The museum's controlled environment and the regular maintenance program drawn up at the end of the intervention and implemented by the CCA will be sufficient to ensure the sculptures' optimal preservation in the future.

The aim of the cultural project for the conservation of the Mont'e Prama sculptures was that of maximum openness to communication, to ensure an integral dissemination of all information relating to the sculptures, including the interventions just described. To raise public awareness and make this extraordinary cultural phenomenon known at regional, national, and international levels, the entire program was structured in such a way as to be always accessible, both in person and remotely. For this reason, the restoration laboratory was extended in the gallery of the Li Punti Center, inside of which workstations were installed in an environment reconstructed on the image of the Mont'e Prama site, complete with vegetation and fragrant essences to give a fourth dimension to the visitor experience (figures 5.12 and 5.13). An aerial balcony allowed visits without time limits or the need to make reservations, and without interfering with the progress of the work. Guided tours were organized and posters were printed, along with brochures and didactic material distributed to visiting school groups. For the first time in a conservation project, a press officer was included as an integral part of the organizational chart, entirely dedicated to communication both on site and through the media.

A web page, www.monteprama.it, was created in Italian, English, and Sardinian, where it was possible to follow the progress of the work, book a guided tour, and enter the photo gallery of the restoration and

FIGURE 5.12 To raise public awareness, the program has been structured so as to be always accessible, in person and remotely.

FIGURE 5.13 The restoration laboratory extends into the gallery of the Li Punti Center. Workstations sit in an environment designed to resemble the Mont'e Prama site, complete with a recreation of the plants and the fragrance.

conservation work. The website was updated weekly for the duration of the project and included press coverage of the sculptures' restorations, in order to keep the public informed of the main news and relevant debates. The video material shot during the course of the work was edited with subtitles in Italian, English, and Sardinian.

The activities that perhaps contributed most to creating a close bond with the public were the visits and the drawing competition for students. Thanks to a program organized at a regional level, primary and secondary schools were invited to visit the laboratory and were welcomed by the conservators at work, who were happy to share their experiences.

Samples of the same material as that of the sculptures were made available to the students, who were given the opportunity to try the cleaning tools on them. The drawing competition, called "the poster I would like,"

FIGURE 5.14 Conservators share their experiences with students from primary and secondary schools who are invited to visit the laboratory.

gave results well above expectations: a number of beautiful drawings were produced, thanks to the creativity of the students and the availability and effort of the teachers, who prepared the visit and continued to elaborate on the experience back in the classroom. Many schoolchildren returned to follow the progress of the work and see the sculptures mounted on the supports, demonstrating a sincere interest in the conservation project and in the history of their own civilization. Similar results elsewhere confirm the public's interest in being involved with and interacting with conservators (figure 5.14).[5]

CONCLUSIONS

The Mont'e Prama—Prenda 'e Zenia Cultural Project was made possible thanks to a perfect synergy between forward-looking public officials and passionate private conservators. In this project some of the essential principles of modern conservation ethics were put into practice, confirming that rigor and method always lead in the desired direction, and that education and training—as in the case of restoration and conservation in Italy—are the cornerstone of a civil society. Methodological principles should always be kept in mind: documentation, knowledge, respect, reversibility, training, recontextualization, communication, and sharing.

Full *documentation* of what was found and what was done was a daily practice throughout the intervention. Photographs, drawings, videos, technical reports, and databases now constitute a rich body of knowledge that is available to all. The study of the artifacts—from their iconographic forms to the execution and finishing techniques, from the traces of destruction to the processes of decay, both in the answers provided and in the questions that are still unresolved—today represents the *knowledge* that has been acquired, which is made available in its entirety to all through the many publications produced.[6] *Respect* for the materials and original shapes and the *reversibility* of what was produced during the intervention are the material inheritance that will allow the completion of the sculptures through the insertion of new finds, without affecting what has been achieved to date. The *training* of young conservators, who in this case included more than ten Sardinian technicians, provided an opportunity for professional growth to talented young people who will deal with the future conservation of the island's cultural heritage. The *recontextualization* of the "Sculptures of Mont'e Prama" as an encompassing phenomenon within the deepest consciousness of the Sardinian people helps to mend that injury generated by over thirty centuries of oblivion. *Communication* means openness to the public and continuous dissemination of the results acquired as tools for producing culture, generating consensus, recontextualizing phenomena, and sharing. Indeed, *sharing* is the goal of this whole operation, at both a regional and a global level—sharing of scientific results and of the cultural and economic benefits that derive from them.

I will never stop reiterating that the sculptures of Mont'e Prama should be read in a universal key, as they are a phenomenon that interests the world. The whole world wants to know them and enjoy them—wants to be surprised by them. Consequently, it wants to visit them within their context, connected to their original environment. The world wants to experience the sculptures, just as it wants to experience what surrounds them today— the Cabras pond, the Sinis peninsula, and all that the territory offers.

Fifteen years have passed since the beginning of the restoration work on the sculptures, and this exhibition has provided an unexpected opportunity to take stock of one of the most important public cultural operations of the beginning of the millennium. Thanks to a series of favorable events—an accidental discovery by a farmer who diligently alerted the authorities, an archaeological excavation conducted by the university and the superintendency, a perfect synergy between enlightened officials and dedicated conservators—the cultural panorama of Sardinia and of the entire world has today been enriched by a foundational origin story.

The destiny of our Giants, however, continues to be characterized by the chiaroscuro tones of the early history of the sculptures. In these ten years many things have happened: new excavation campaigns (2014–2018) have brought to light more than 4,500 new sculpture fragments, yet these fragments again lie in the darkness of warehouses; much new and interesting scientific information came from the archaeological investigation, yet some questions, such as the precise dating of the sculptures, their original location, their relationship with the tombs, and the reasons for their destruction, remain unanswered.[7] Although the sculptures are from a single army, they have been divided into two battalions and exhibited in the museums of Cabras and Cagliari, deprived of the historical message that the power of a unitary vision in the original context within the natural environment on the shores of the Cabras pond would allow.[8]

The creation of open and reversible supports, suitable for accommodating new finds, and the availability of the conservators who hold the memory of the fragments would have allowed the completion of the restoration; yet the restoration has stopped and the sculptures remain incomplete. What was born to be a magnificent cultural operation, strengthened by the power to expand the archaeological knowledge of the western Mediterranean, is today in fact one of the most sensational unfinished projects in the history of world archaeology and one of the largest missed opportunities for economic redemption in a region.[9] Nonetheless, in recent years the sculptures of Mont'e Prama have virtually traveled the world, from America to China and across half of Europe; they have been appreciated by scholars and connoisseurs. The cultural program for the sculptures' conservation has received recognition in Europe and around the world (figure 5.15).[10] It is necessary

FIGURE 5.15 The Mont'e Prama conservation won the 2015 EU Prize for Cultural Heritage/Europa Nostra Award, presented by Norway's Crown Prince.

to wait until the power emanating from the sculptures of Mont'e Prama, embodied in their very nature and in their international fame, paves the way for the achievement of the interrupted objectives. Recent events suggest cautious optimism. The establishment of the Fondazione Mont'e Prama, requested by the ministry, represents an explicit recognition of the universal value of the sculptures. This foundation brings together the ministry, the region of Sardinia, and the Comune of Cabras and has as its statutory objective the development of a cultural plan for the enhancement of the sculptures and their territory of origin.

It is hoped that the underlying intent is to complete the restoration and exhibit the collection in a single venue, the Cabras museum. If so, we might think that the long march of the sculptures of Mont'e Prama is close to the point of arrival, and that in the near future we will be able to see them all together, restored, on the shores of the Cabras pond, restoring pride and well-being to the descendants of those who gave rise, three thousand years ago, to this extraordinary cultural phenomenon.

<hr />

Translated by Jane Botsford Johnson and Francesco de Angelis.

NOTES

1. For the archaeological survey, see L. Usai, "Mont'e Prama, prima del restauro," in *Le sculture di Mont'e Prama, conservazione e restauro,* ed. A. Boninu and A. Costanzi Cobau (Rome: Gangemi, 2014).

2. Among the countless direct initiatives in defense of Sardinia's archaeological heritage, Antonietta Boninu was the engine of the conservation intervention of the sculptures of Mont'e Prama, during which she worked daily and tirelessly in the role of site manager. The intervention was carried out thanks to an agreement on program management between the Ministero per I Beni e le Attività Culturali and the Regione Autonoma della Sardegna, Finanziamento 2005 and Atto Integrativo 2006, APQ 2005, Progetto SAR BC2-10; APQ 2005, A.I.2006 Progetto SAR BD-05.

3. Since the practice of grouping specialist restoration interventions with more general public works projects came into force, and therefore since the criterion of maximum discount tenders was introduced, the CCA has not participated in tenders of this kind in Italy, as we believe that the delicacy of the matter and the uniqueness of the interventions (as in surgical medicine) require the use of skilled, not low-cost, labor. This explains why the CCA has worked almost exclusively abroad since the 1990s.

4. A. Boninu, "Per le sculture di Mont'e Prama oportet rationem operis instituere," in *Tra Ionio e Tirreno. Orizzonti di Archeologia. Omaggio ad Elena Lattanzi,* ed. R. Spadea, F. Lo Schiavo, and M. L. Lazzarini (Rome: Scienze e Lettere, 2020), 157–172.

5. R. Nardi, "Open Hearth Restoration: Raising the Awareness of the Public," *ICOM* (1995), series 1, 9–11; R. Nardi, "Going Public: A New Approach to Conservation Education. Involving the Public in Conservation," *Museum International, ICOM* (Paris), 44–50; R. Nardi, "Tourism Management of Archaeological Sites Within an Urban Context: A Balanced Compromise Between Preventive Conservation and Cultural Use," *Proceedings of the 4th European Commission Conference on Research for Protection, Conservation,*

and Enhancement of Cultural Heritage; Opportunities for European Enterprises, Strasbourg, November 22–24, 2000, 168–75.

6. See, for example, A. Boninu and A. Costanzi Cobau, *Le sculture di Mont'e Prama, conservazione e restauro* (Rome: Gangemi, 2014).

7. The new excavation campaigns were directed by Alessandro Usai for the Soprintendenza Archeologica and by Raimondo Zucca for the Università degli studi di Sassari.

8. L. Usai, ed., *Le sculture di Mont'e Prama, La Mostra, Roma* (2014): "La divisione delle sculture nei due istituti museali e in sedi distanti, da ritenersi inopinata, improvvida e incomprensibile, desta notevoli perplessità. Sicuramente non favorisce l'attività della conservazione, anzi, comporta complicazioni operative, dilata i tempi necessari e ne aumenta i costi."

9. R. Nardi, "Does Culture Produce Bread?," in *Proceedings of the 16th The Best in Heritage Conference*, Dubrovnik, Croatia, September 28–20, 2017, ed. Tomislav S. Sola and Luca Cipek, European Heritage Association/The Best in Heritage, Zagreb, Croatia, 38–41.

10. From Boninu, "Per le sculture di Mont'e Prama oportet rationem operis instituere":

   – EU Prize for Cultural Heritage 2015, European Prize for Cultural Heritage, Europa Nostra Awards 2015, Oslo, June 11, 2015' 263 projects from 29 countries presented. First prize. Motivation of the jury: the jury was fascinated by the complexity of this restoration project, and struck by its importance in revealing this underrated culture. The assembly of the pieces, performed without deep penetration of the original stone, avoiding the use of drills or the insertion of different materials, will allow changes and additions to the images of the statues in the future. All the restoration operations were carried out publicly, with the public able to visit the works in progress. The importance for the local population is evident, enhancing their identification with the inhabitants who preceded them on this large island.

   – 2015 National Innovation Award for the important enhancement of an intervention for the conservation and restoration of archaeological assets, which simultaneously aimed at facilitating their use by citizens.

   – The Best in Heritage, Dubrovnik, Croatia, September 24–25, 2016, recognizes the conservation of the sculptures as the best project in the world. Beyond the specific motivations, the acknowledgments awarded at the national, European, and world levels indicate the singularity of the conservation project of the Mont'e Prama sculptures, for the setting, the method, the solutions conceived and implemented, and the results.

The Illicit Trafficking of Sardinian Cultural Objects

GIUDITTA GIARDINI, Manhattan District Attorney's Office

The archaeologist and politician Giovanni Lilliu once said, "There are more Nuragic bronzes abroad than in Sardinia."[1] In addition, the majority of Sardinian bronzes that left the island between the 1980s and the 1990s were proceeds of illegal excavations. The illicit trafficking of antiquities in Sardinia and elsewhere is not a new phenomenon, but it still makes newspaper headlines. To explain how the supply chain of looted antiquities works, this essay provides an overview of the illicit trafficking ring active in Italy in the 1980s and uncovered around 1995. It then focuses on the supply chain of Sardinian antiquities: from tomb robbers to middlemen, and from middlemen to international dealers. The study aims to demonstrate the presence of looting of archeological sites in Sardinia and the impact it has on archaeology and scientific studies at large; it also shows most likely looted objects and affected areas. After briefly introducing Italian laws protecting undiscovered antiquities, the essay presents the case of a Sardinian bronze statuette of the archer of Sant'Antioco Island as an excellent example of cultural diplomacy. The essay strongly advocates for the creation of regional "red" lists of Italian antiquities at risk, mirroring those Red Lists published by the International Council of Museums (ICOM) for countries with cultural heritage at risk.

HOW ILLICIT TRAFFICKING WORKS:
THE ITALIAN CASE STUDY

In 1994 a raid in Munich, Germany, on antiquities dealer Antonio Savoca's residence recovered vases and records implicating Pasquale Camera—a retired captain of the Guardia di Finanza (Italian financial police)—in the trafficking of the vases.[2] In 1995, after Camera died in a car accident, the police found incriminating documents and photos of looted antiquities in his vehicle. That material led to seventy additional searches, including a search of Danilo Zicchi's apartment in Rome in September 1995 that uncovered a single page in Camera's handwriting of what appeared to be an organizational chart, known as the *organigramma* (organigram; see figure 6.1).[3]

The organigram presents a view of the antiquities trade within Italy as envisaged by Camera in the early 1990s. The Paris-based U.S. dealer Robert Hecht occupies a central place on the chart, with arrows linking him to collectors and museums in the United States and France; to major antiquities dealers Nikos Koutoulakis, Eli Borowsky, and Frieda Tchacos; and to the Bolivian antiquities collector George Ortiz. Under Hecht's name are listed Gianfranco Becchina, Giacomo Medici, and other now-convicted traffickers, including many *tombaroli* (tomb raiders), and the areas covered by tombaroli squads. An arrow from Gianfranco Becchina points directly to the trafficker Mario Bruno. Bruno had been an active Italian trafficker from the 1970s until his death in 1993. According to the organigram, he covered the areas of "North Italy, Rome, Lazio, Campania, Puglia, Sardinia and Sicily."[4] Sardinia is therefore a source of looted antiquities, illegally excavated by tombaroli and shipped to Mario Bruno, who would offer them for sale to the convicted dealer Gianfranco Becchina.[5] As the chart shows, Becchina had enough connections and the means to place the objects in major collections, auction houses, and museums.

From bottom to top, the organigram illustrates the supply chain of looted antiquities, giving an idea of how antiquities trafficking worked in Italy between the 1980s and the 1990s. Archaeological objects are illegally excavated by tomb robbers overnight. Tombaroli move around in squads of five or six people, some preferring to dig pottery, others, for instance, specializing in marble sculptures, architectonic fragments, and tombstones.

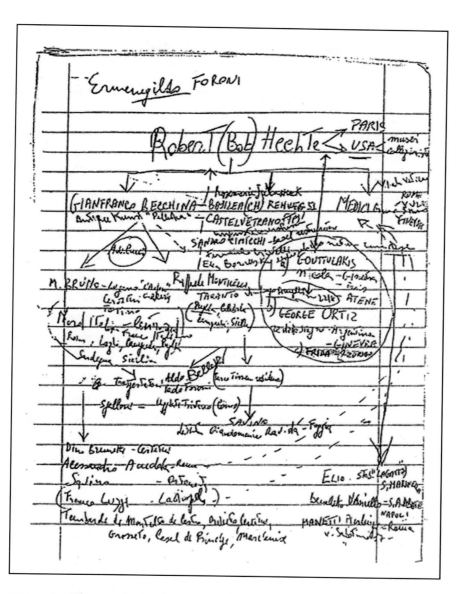

FIGURE 6.1 The organizational chart created by Pasquale Camera and found in the Rome apartment of Danilo Zicchi.

Marble objects are heavier and require strength and sophisticated tools to facilitate the extraction of the antiquities from the earth. Tombaroli squads operate in different areas to avoid overlapping and finding empty—because already excavated—tombs. Active tombaroli break into tombs about twice per month or every ten days.[6] They even trespass on property owned by farmers to secure the booty.

The proceeds of the illegal activities carried out by tombaroli squads are managed by *capozone* (middlemen), usually former tombaroli who coordinate the sales of antiquities in a given area. Dealers who do not have a direct source of antiquities turn to a *capozona* to find pieces.[7] If the pieces are not sold directly to a dealer, the *capozona* finds a buyer abroad. Traffickers active in Italy in the 1990s brought looted antiquities to Switzerland to have them stored in free-port rooms not subject to control, pending a good offer. To smuggle antiquities across borders, traffickers placed the most valuable pieces in "diplomatic luggage," not subject to check at customs, and hid average-quality pieces in boxes filled with other goods stuck in trucks and cars. Voluminous antiquities were broken into pieces to facilitate transit. To allow successful restoration, figurative vases were broken across the unpainted parts. Looted objects were photographed before and after restoration using Polaroid cameras for rapid and private development. The pieces were entrusted to corrupt restorers who did not ask questions on their provenance. Once antiquities were restored, they were offered for sale to auction houses, major museums, and reputable collectors. Their passage in a public sale or the prolonged presence of an unprovenanced piece in a well-known collection and its subsequent loan to major museums contributed to laundering "dirty" antiquities.

A perfect example of how the supply chain of illicit trafficking worked is represented by the sale of the famous Euphronios krater to the Metropolitan Museum of New York. In 1971 a group of tombaroli excavated the krater in Cerveteri and immediately reached out to Giacomo Medici, who went to see it in person. After Medici and Robert Hecht decided to buy the krater in partnership, the vase was illegally exported to Zurich. In Switzerland, the third member of the conspiracy, Fritz Burki, restored it. Hecht took photos of the vase and sent them to major museums. Finally, in 1972, the Metropolitan Museum decided to buy the work of Euphronios for one million dollars.[8] Eventually, in 2006, the krater was returned to Italy as part of an agreement between the Italian Republic and the New York museum.[9]

SARDINIAN *TOMBAROLI, CAPOZONE,* AND DEALERS

One of the most prolific middlemen of Sardinian antiquities was Pietro Mocci, also known as the Sardinian Medici or il Nibbio.[10] There is little information on Mocci's life. He was an expert on Nuragic bronzes, and his client list included the collector George Ortiz, Gianfranco Becchina, and well-known U.S. museums and galleries. In the late 1980s Mocci was involved in a car crash on the Strada Statale 131 Carlo San Felice, the major road in Sardinia, and died on the spot. In his car, the police found 100 million old lire (almost 52,000 euros), the proceeds of the sale of looted antiquities, and a planner containing names, addresses, and areas under the responsibility of various personalities linked to the antiquities black market, including local grave robbers and international traffickers. What incriminated Mocci, however, were the name "Gianfranco Becchina" and Becchina's link to his Swiss gallery written on the planner. Lieutenant Roberto Lai, from the Italian Carabinieri Tutela Patrimonio Culturale (TPC), recognized the connection with the Helvetic territory as being problematic. At that time, many antiquities were illegally excavated and brought to Switzerland to find a buyer. Later, in 1995, the presence of Gianfranco Becchina's name on Pasquale Camera's organigram confirmed Lieutenant Lai's thesis.

The organigram also made it clear that the Sardinian territory was one of the major sources of looted antiquities in the antiquities black market. According to this document, it was Mario Bruno, one of the most prolific Italian traffickers, who supplied Sardinian antiquities to the convicted Italian dealer Giovanni Franco Becchina. Based on the chart, Bruno controlled areas in both central northern and southern Italy and had connections with nearly every major trafficker in the country. He resided in both Cerveteri (Italy) and Lugano (Switzerland), taking advantage of his dual locations to quickly move antiquities across the Swiss border. Over the years, Bruno had been reported multiple times by municipalities across Italy for receiving and selling stolen and looted cultural property.[11]

Mario Bruno was not the only middleman Becchina was in touch with for the purchase of Sardinian antiquities. The *capozona* Pietro Mocci features prominently in the Becchina archive, namely, the entire universe of photographs and documents seized from Becchina during the search of his gallery and free-port rooms. After Mocci's tragic death, Mario Deiana tried to fill his shoes. Deiana sent letters to Mocci's old clients, including Becchina and George Ortiz, where he introduced himself as the heir of Pietro Mocci,[12] explaining for international dealers how to launder his dirty antiquities by creating fake provenance.[13] Deiana and Mocci acted as intermediaries: they were in touch with Sardinian tombaroli and could easily get possession of bronze statuettes of warriors, archers, tribal leaders, and vessels. Intermediaries are an essential ring on the smuggling chain; they are in touch with tombaroli, know interested buyers to secure good deals, and at the same time have deep knowledge of the objects offered for sale. In one of his letters, for instance, Deiana showed a great knowledge of the Nuragic bronzes he offered for sale. He explained to Becchina that the standard height for a Nuragic bronze is 10 centimeters and that there are fewer, rarer, and very beautiful pieces 18–20 centimeters in height.[14] Deiana knew the market well: in his correspondence with the Basel-based dealer, he explained that idols from the Upper Neolithic or the Lower Neolithic, dating back to more than four or five thousand years ago and found in caves and domus, would sell better than Sardinian Neolithic vases.

In June 2021 the prosecutor of Lanusei (Nuoro) charged thirty-four tombaroli and middlemen with the crime of conspiracy to conduct illicit excavation, theft of property owned by the state, and illegal export of antiquities. The scheme is always the same: the tombaroli squads active in Ogliastra were in touch with a *sardo-ogliastrino* emigrant, the middleman, living in France who orchestrated the sale of the antiquities on the French antiquities market.[15]

SARDINIAN LOOTED PIECES

In general, intermediaries have a price list for looted pieces to sell abroad to antiquities traffickers. The price list is based on their personal experience, auction sale results, and knowledge of deals made by their competitors for similar objects. Mocci and Deiana sold mostly Nuragic bronzes to international traffickers and clients. Nuragic bronzes sell well because they are rare, as they are typical of Sardinia. The most valuable Sardinian treasures are stone medallions engraved with idols from the Nuragic period. In one of his letters, Deiana explains that stone medallions are very hard to find, and there seem to be just two examples in two Sardinian museums. Coins and pottery are common; hence they do not sell as well as bronze figurines.

Nuragic Bronzes

In 1990 Becchina sold thirty-two Nuragic bronzes to the Merrin Gallery, one of the most popular galleries in New York. The bronzes included statuettes of animals, priestesses, warriors, and vessels, dating from 900 to 600 BCE, for eight billion old lire (circa 400,000 euros). Among the objects seized from the Swiss dealers was a group of Sardinian bronzes: anthropomorphic bronzes, a vessel, haxes, and cauldron appliques. In 2013, while discussing the restitution of Becchina's Sardinian pieces to Italy, Marcello Madau recalled the Genevan exhibition titled *L'Art del peuples italiques. 3000 à 300 a.C.*, which took place in the early 1990s. According to Madau, the exhibition featured "many looted Sardinian antiquities and fakes as well." The thirty-two Sardinian pieces on display were almost all bronzes. Twenty-four lacked any provenance indication, and for eight the provenance only read *provincia di Nuoro* (province of Nuoro).[17]

In June 2021 the Carabinieri TPC raided the houses of two tomb robbers caught excavating archeological sites near Cagliari. During the execution of a search warrant in the tombaroli's houses, they found more than a thousand antiquities. Among the seized objects there were six very rare Nuragic vessels, a Nuragic ram-headed prothome, the bust of a Nuragic warrior with a dagger, and an anthropomorphic figurine.

To give a sense of how highly Nuragic antiquities are valued, in 2012 the Royal Athena Galleries in New York offered six Nuragic antiquities, which were part of the "Sardinian Iberian Catalogue." In 2017, a Sardinian bronze worshiper went for $125,000 at a Christie's sale (figure 6.2). The sale outraged many Sardinians, considering that the provenance of the piece was linked to Switzerland. And on July 7, 2022, the Manhattan District

FIGURE 6.2 This Sardinian bronze worshiper sold in 2017 at Christie's New York for $125,000 (above the estimate of $50,000–$70,000).

Attorney's Office returned 142 cultural objects that had been looted from Italy and were illegally present in New York. Among the pieces returned was one held by hedge fund manager Michael Steinhardt: a 14-inch-tall Sardinian idol, dated 2500–2000 BCE and valued at over one million dollars.

Neolithic and Nuragic Jewels

Nuragic jewels and votive and religious ornaments are not easy to find. In Becchina's booty, the Carabinieri TPC found decorated buttons. In the houses of the two tombaroli raided in the summer of 2021, the Carabinieri found a Neolithic bone necklace (sixth to third millenium BCE) and a bronze medallion decorated with leaves and birds.

Weapons

Religion and war played a strong role in Nuragic society. This is reflected in the number of weapons found in Sardinia. From the Becchina collection, the Carabinieri TPC seized and returned an extraordinary Nuragic dagger with a jeweled hilt. More recently, dozens of Neolithic and Nuragic lithic axes and maces were found in the houses of the two tombaroli near Cagliari.

Etruscan–Corithian Pottery

Among the objects that originated from Sardinia are antiquities that reached the island because they were bartered or purchased by inhabitants there. The so-called Nuragic group seized from Becchina included a villanovan (hence early Etruscan) razor. The presence of an Etrusan object in a Nuragic group (made exclusively of bronze statuettes and prothomes) was not a coincidence. Chances are high that the razor belonged in the same tomb as the bronze pieces.

Phoenician Glass

In December 2021 the Manhattan District Attorney's Office returned to Italy a Phoenician glass pendant in the shape of a head. The Italian trafficker

Edoardo Almagià sold the pendant to the Cleveland Museum around 1993.[18] The Manhattan Prosecutor's Office seized the object from the museum. The pendant head is very similar to the little glass heads decorating the Olbia glass necklace (figures 6.3 and 6.4) found in 1937 at the necropolis of Funtana Noa in tomb 24, dated between 400 and 300 BCE. Glass obtained with core-glass processing (ointments, pendants, or elements of necklaces) is not the only valuable Phoenician glass; faiences, such as sigillary plaques, amulets, and scarabs, are also valuable. Glass was produced in workshops in the main cities of Phoenicia. Phoenicians exported their manufactures to all their colonies, including Sardinian ones: Nora, Tharros, Cagliari, Sant'Antioco, and Bithia.

Roman Coins

About 550 bronze and silver coins dating from the Phoenician era up to Roman Republican and Imperial time were found in the houses of two tombaroli in summer 2021. Some of the coins were minted in Punic-Sardinian mints (300 BCE); others, such as the so-called Roman *asse del Sardus Pater* (100 BCE) and Byzantine-Sardinian coins (600–700 CE), were minted on Sardinia.

In general, considering Italian and international case law and the results of auction sales, it is easy to identify the types of antiquities that are most easily excavated and exported illegally from Sardinia. This observation needs to be validated by expert archaeologists.

ITALIAN LAW PROTECTING CULTURAL HERITAGE

Objects found under the Italian ground or on the Italian seabed belong *ipso iure* to the inalienable patrimony of the Italian state.[19] Therefore antiquities illegally excavated or legally excavated but illegally retained in Sardinia or elsewhere in Italian territory are considered stolen. Italy has probably one of the oldest patrimony laws protecting national antiquities in the world. The safeguarding and preservation of Italy's artistic heritage has been a key priority of the unified Italian government since 1861.

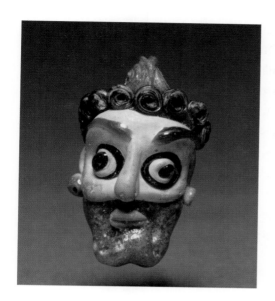

FIGURE 6.3 The Carthaginian glass head that Edoardo Almagià sold to the Cleveland Museum around 1993; it was recently seized and returned to Italy.

FIGURE 6.4 The Phoenician glass necklace from Olbia (*National Archaeological Museum of Cagliari*).

A cultural heritage law concerning, inter alia, all antiquities found in Italy in 1902 established that "collections of objects of art and antiquity, monuments and small objects of artistic and archaeological importance . . . belonging to ecclesiastical bodies of any nature, those that adorn churches and dependent places or any other public buildings are inalienable. Also inalienable are collections and individual objects of art and antiquity that are not part of collections."[20]

Ownership of antiquities not yet excavated was vested in the Italian state in 1909 by Article 15(3) of Law No. 364, June 20, 1909, which states that "things found belong to the State."[21] The national patrimony law was updated by Law No. 1089 of June 1, 1939, on the Protection of Objects of Artistic and Historic Interest, commonly referred to as "the Bottai Law," named after the late minister of education, Giuseppe Bottai.[22] The Bottai Law not only claimed national ownership of undiscovered antiquities ("le cose ritrovate appartengono allo Stato") but also regulated the excavation and exportation—a legal regime that protects archaeological sites and objects, vesting ownership in the state (articles 44, 46–47, and 49). The law vested title in the Republic of Italy to antiquities found by chance during archaeological excavations or outside of them within the borders of Italy ("le cose scoperte fortuitamente appartengono allo Stato," article 49) and required state-approved licenses for the exportation of archaeological objects (articles 35–41). Sixty years later the Act on Cultural Property and Landscape (*Testo Unico delle Disposizioni Legislative in Materia di Beni Culturali ed Ambientali*) of 1999 reaffirmed in article 88 the provisions of articles 44–49 of the Bottai Law.[23] Today the Italian patrimony law is Legislative Decree No. 42 of January 22, 2004, the so-called Code of Cultural Property and Landscape, or simply "the Urbani Code," named after the late minister of culture, Giuliano Urbani.[24] The Urbani Code protects all "moveable and immovable things of artistic, historic, archaeological or ethnological interest" (article 10). Based on article 91, all things indicated in article 10 "by anyone and in any way found in the subsoil or on the seabed, belong to the State and, depending on whether they are immovable or movable, are part of the nondisposable patrimony of the State, pursuant to articles 822 and 826 of the [1942] Italian Civil Code."[25]

Following the ratification of the 2017 Council of Europe Convention on Offenses relating to Cultural Property, with Law No. 22 of March 9, 2022, Italy undertook a reform of the Italian Penal Code.[26] The reform, which introduced a new title for crimes against cultural objects (Articles 518bis–518vicies and 707bis), aims to improve and facilitate the fight against illicit trafficking of antiquities.[27]

THE LOSS

Illicit trafficking of Sardinian antiquities, especially those from the Nuragic period, about which very little is known, contributes to erasing the memory of the ancient populations who inhabited the Italian island. It is as if the grave robbers and traffickers had torn pages from the book of the history of Italy or, in this case, the book of the history of Sardinia. From the information obtained from the cases under scrutiny, it was possible to ascertain that the illicit trafficking of Sardinian antiquities concerned particularly small and medium-sized Nuragic bronzes. The clandestine excavation of the bronzes and their entry into private collections, without being published, prevents archaeologists from gathering important information, not only on the place of burial and the places where the pieces are found, but also on the features of the statuettes. In fact, fundamental in the reconstruction of the features and the identity of the Giants of Mont'e Prama were the bronzes that reproduced archers and warriors in similar poses (figure 6.5).[28] Sadly, the identity of the giant with round eyes and a shield on his head has been difficult to reconstruct. It seems that no similar statue has yet been found, or perhaps it was clandestinely excavated and sold to a private collector.

In the trial of the convicted trafficker Gianfranco Becchina, court experts suggested that in order to find at least one of the objects—including Sardinian objects—of the kind of the six thousand seized from Becchina, the tombaroli would have had to dig up and therefore ruin forever at least twenty ancient tombs.[29]

These two examples are necessary to illustrate the damage that antiquities trafficking causes, not only to archaeology and the progress of science in general but also to the territory, the environment, and local communities.

RESTITUTION CASES

Circling back to Pietro Mocci's tragic departure, thanks to the clues contained in the planner found in his car, Lieutenant Lai identified the thread of the looted bronze statue of an archer known as the Archer of Sant' Antioco.[30] Among the documents seized from Mocci were volumes of

FIGURE 6.5 A bronze statuette of an archer stands alongside a colossal stone archer (*National Archaeological Museum of Cagliari*).

FIGURE 6.6 The bronze archer of Sant'Antioco illegally excavated in Grutt'e Acqua, a Nuragic complex located on the island of Sant'Antioco.

Polaroids, one of them containing photos of a bronze statuette, about 22 centimeters high, of a man, perhaps an archer, in a praying pose, encrusted with dirt. The photos show the piece from three different angles. The archer had a large bow on his shoulder and wore an armored bodice and a helmet with two long horns reaching upward (figure 6.6). Attached to the photo was a note: "Grutt'e Acqua, Sant'Antioco." It was a Nuragic bronze statue, forged on Plumbaria Island about three thousand years ago. Grutt'e Acqua is the name of the Nuragic complex located on the island of Sant'Antioco.

The bronze archer seemed impossible to locate until it appeared in the 1991 acquisitions bulletin of the Cleveland Museum. Thanks to the photo contained in the bulletin, it was possible to declare that the piece at the museum was the same one portrayed in Mocci's Polaroids. With international rogatory letters requesting subpoenas, the Italian prosecutor found out from the museum that the piece entered the museum's collection in the late 1960s. It had been illegally excavated before 1960 in Sant'Antioco and illegally exported from Sardinia. After some obscure passing among hands, the bronze statuette was purchased by the Cleveland Museum. After years of diatribes and negotiations that put pressure on the museum's director and involved the Ohio attorney general, an agreement was finally negotiated through diplomatic channels in 2009 on the return of the piece to Sardinia. The museum had strongly opposed the return, claiming good faith, ownership rights over the archer, and the passage of time. When the procedures for the return of the bronze archer began, the museum put two conditions on the restitution of the piece: the bronze should be exhibited in the same place where it was illegally excavated (Sant'Antioco), and the museum wanted to receive on loan from the Italian Ministry of Culture a number of pieces of the same number and value as those returned.[31] Today the Nuragic archer is exhibited in the Ferruccio Barreca Archaeological Museum in Sant'Antioco.[32]

CONCLUSIONS AND PROPOSAL

Recent arrests and trials of Sardinian tombaroli and middlemen show that the illicit trafficking of antiquities in Sardinia has never stopped. If the demand for antiquities is high, the offer never drops, and looters will always find ways to satisfy the desires of rich museums and wealthy collectors. Unlike the market for Etruscan and Greek objects, the demand for Sardinian antiquities is very peculiar: there is a robust demand for a specific type of antiquities. Nuragic bronze statuettes and weapons and Phoenician glass are high sellers. Italian patrimony law, however, prohibits the export of such bronzes and glass, unless the possessor can prove to have acquired and exported the objects before the entry into force of the 1939 law. While the severity of the patrimony law restricts the legal market for Sardinian antiquities, the scarcity of the objects increases their prices at auction. The prospect of making easy money by selling what can be easily found underground seduces poor Sardinian people. Although the behavior of grave robbers cannot be justified in any way, the Italian state must study the situation and take measures.

Recently, the Manhattan District Attorney's Office has returned to the Republic of Italy more than two hundred looted antiquities that were circulating in the New York market. Nonetheless, Italy cannot continue to rely only on the virtuosity of foreign prosecutor offices, cultural diplomacy, and the tireless work of the Carabinieri. The Italian government has to find ways to educate first-time buyers, collectors, and dealers. Therefore this essay advocates the creation of lists of cultural objects most likely to be looted in each Italian region. The Sardinian case study and the list of Sardinian objects will be the perfect prototypes. The list of Sardinian antiquities at risk would have to briefly explain to the public why a red list (like those promulgated by the International Council of Museums) is necessary for Sardinian antiquities and the need for the state to protect its objects. Antiquities should be divided among utensils used for writing, sculpted objects (stelae, statuettes, busts, etc.), bronze objects, architectural elements, vessels and containers, coins and seals, accessories and tools, and jewelry.[33]

Italian and foreign museums as well as Italian and foreign dealers and collectors could check the lists to get a sense of what antiquities are most likely to be looted and refuse to buy them. Red lists should be easily available online. Such lists will also encourage dealers, collectors, and auction houses to report to the Carabinieri TPC items offered for sale that lack provenance.

NOTES

1. M. Madau, "Di un'altra razza, son tombarolo," *Il Manifesto Sardo*, September 1, 2009, https://www.manifestosardo.org/di-un%E2%80%99altra-razza-son-tombarolo/; M. Madau, "Fermiamo il Furto d'Identità," *La Nuova Sardegna*, December 22, 2013, https://ricerca.gelocal.it/lanuovasardegna/archivio/lanuovasardegna/2013/12/22/OL_02_03.html.

2. P. Watson and C. Todeschini, *The Medici Conspiracy: The Illicit Journey of Looted Antiquities—from Italy's Tomb Raiders to the World's Greatest Museums* (New York: PublicAffairs, 2007), 6.

3. The organigram is available at Neil Brodie, "Organigram," Trafficking Culture, August 21, 2012, https://traffickingculture.org/encyclopedia/case-studies/organigram/.

4. Watson and Todeschini, *The Medici Conspiracy*, 17.

5. Information on Giovanni Franco (Gianfranco) Becchina is from United Nations Office on Drugs and Crime, SHERLOC, https://sherloc.unodc.org/cld/uploads/res/case-law -doc/traffickingculturalpropertycrimetype/ita/case_g__becchina_html/Becchina.pdf, accessed January 3, 2022.

6. "On average, I break into a tomb every ten days," explains Antonio Induno. "First, I identify an unearthed site. I go for a walk, as we're doing now, and I choose a spot. Then I do a survey of the tomb by piercing the earth with spilloni (long metal poles) and working out where the entrance is, how large the tomb is, how deeply it lies buried. I mark the spot with a pile of stones, a plastic bag, anything will do, and I come back with my men at night." C. Ruiz, "My Life as a Tombarolo: *The Art Newspaper* Goes Underground in the World of Illicit Archaeology," *ArtNewspaper*, February 28, 2001, https:// www.theartnewspaper.com/2001/03/01/my-life-as-a-tombarolo-the-art-ewspaper -goes-underground-in-the-world-of-illicit-archaeology.

7. To give an example, Giacomo Medici, the worst known Italian antiquities trafficker of all time, started his apprenticeship working for the capozona of the area of old Etruria, the so-called *farmacista* (pharmacist), before moving to Switzerland to work for dealer Elie Borowski. Watson and Todeschini, *The Medici Conspiracy*, 167.

8. T. Hoving, *The Chase the Capture: Collecting at the Metropolitan Museum* (New York: Metropolitan Museum of Art, 1975), 40–56.

9. https://www.metmuseum.org/press/news/2006/statement-by-the-metropolitan -museum-of-art-on-its-agreement-with-italian-ministry-of-culture.

10. The Carabinieri TPC and the late prosecutor Paolo Giorgio Freri first found out about Pietro Mocci during the investigation *Theseus*, named after the subject—Theseus and the Minotaurus—involving a beautiful corinthian black figure amphora, at the criminal trial against antiquities trafficker Gianfranco Becchina.

11. In 1992 Bruno again came under the radar of the Carabinieri TPC, for his role in receiving and selling the *Triade Capitolina*, a rare marble antiquity looted from Italy. He died in Lugano, Switzerland, in 1993.

12. Madau, "Di un'altra razza, son tombarolo" and "Fermiamo il furto d'identità." F. Isman, *Predatori dell'Arte Perduta* (Skira, 2009), 136–37.

13. *Provenance* is a term of art in the art business. It refers to the history of the ownership of a work of art. Information may come from a range of sources, including contemporary descriptions, inventories of collections, auction sale catalogues, data bases, and *catalogues raisonnés*.

14. The information on the trafficking of Sardinian cultural objects is the result of an interview to the late assistant prosecutor Paolo Giorgio Ferri, personally conducted via Zoom, in February 2020. F. Isman, *Predatori dell'Arte Perduta*.

15. "Operazione 'Dea Madre': 34 denunce per scavi clandestini, armi e droga," Cagliaripad, June 29, 2021, https://www.cagliaripad.it/539283/operazione-dea-madre-34-denunce -per-scavi-clandestini-armi-e-droga/.

16. Madau also recalls that the Carabinieri TPC found a drawing of an extraordinary bronze askòs from the Nuraghe Nurdòle of Orani, similar to one exhibited in Geneva, in the possession of a group of traffickers. Madau, "Di un'altra razza, son tombarolo."

17. The provenance read: "Professor A. G., Lausanne, acquired in the 1950s; acquired by the current owner in Switzerland, 1998." See Christies, "A Sardinian Bronze Worshiper Circa 8th Century B.C.," https://www.christies.com/lot/lot-6067620, accessed January 16, 2022.

18. The term *trafficker* is here employed because Edoardo Almagià sold stolen Italian antiquities to his clients. The confiscation order for such antiquities was upheld by the Supreme Court in Sent. Cass. Pen. Sez.3^ 22/10/2015 Sentenza n.42458.

19. See article 91 of Legislative Decree No. 42, January 22, 2004, *Codice dei beni culturali e del paesaggio*, https://www.normattiva.it/uri-res/N2Ls?urn:nir:stato:decreto.legislativo:2004 -01-22;42.

20. The first antiquities law covering the modern state of Italy after its unification was enacted in 1902 when the Italian state passed Law No. 185, which stipulates that movable objects that have archaeological or artistic value are subject to the provision of the law (article 1).

21. Law No. 364, June 20, 1909, *sulle antichità e le belle arti*, https://www.normattiva.it/uri -res/N2Ls?urn:nir:stato:legge:1909-06-20;364@originale.

22. Law No. 1089, June 1, 1939, *sulla Tutela delle cose d'interesse artistico o storico*, https://www .normattiva.it/uri-res/N2Ls?urn:nir:stato:legge:1939-06-01;1089@originale.

23. Legislative Decree No. 490, October 29, 1999, *Testo Unico delle Disposizioni Legislative in Materia di Beni Culturali ed Ambientali 1999*, https://www.normattiva.it/uri-res /N2Ls?urn:nir:stato:decreto.legislativo:1999-10-29;490. Even before the adoption of the *Testo Unico* in 1979, the Italian Supreme Court similarly found that such works belong to the state (Cass. civ., I, July 13, 1979, n. 4081, GC, 1979, 2043).

24. See article 91 of Legislative Decree of January 22, 2004.

25. The convention was adopted in Nicosia on May 19, 2017. See "Council of Europe Convention on Offences Relating to Cultural Property," https://rm.coe.int/1680710435. Legge 9 marzo 2022, n. 22, "Disposizioni in materia di reati contro il patrimonio culturale" (GU n.68 del 22-03-2022), https://www.normattiva.it/uri-res/N2Ls?urn:nir:stato:legge: 2022;22.

26. Titolo VIII-bis, Dei delitti contro il patrimonio culturale.

27. Royal Decree No. 262, March 16, 1942, Approvazione del testo del Codice civile, https://www.normattiva.it/atto/caricaDettaglioAtto?atto.dataPubblicazioneGazzetta=1942-04-04&atto.codiceRedazionale=042U0262&atto.articolo.numero=0&qId=f9ab1d9e-33d6-4950-bbf8-abfcd45d8e5e&tabID=0.2494168950430744&title=lbl.dettaglioAtto.

28. The Giants of Mont'e Prama are ancient stone sculptures dating back to the Nuragic civilization. They were discovered in 1974 next to a necropolis near Mont'e Prama, Cabras, Sardinia.

29. D. Rizzo and M. Pellegrini, *The Italian Archaeological Heritage Abroad: Agreements, Debates and Indifference* (Rome: Edizioni CaFoscari, 2021), https://edizionicafoscari.unive.it/media/pdf/books/978-88-6969-518-6/978-88-6969-518-6-ch-05_tdFSBPD.pdf; T. Cevoli, *Senza Voce*, Centro Studi Criminologici, https://www.criminologi.com/web/wp-content/uploads/2020/05/T_Cevoli_Storia_senza_voce_CSC_2020_EBOOK_EDIZIONE_2.pdf, accessed January 3, 2022.

30. F. Pitzanti, "Archeologia. Da Sant'Antioco a Cleveland e ritorno: il bronzetto dell'arciere ritrovato, by Roberto Lai, Francesca Pitzanti intervista By Roberto Lai," *Tentazioni della Penna*, November 12, 2021, http://www.tentazionidellapenna.com/rassegna-stampa/55-rassegna-stampa-nazionale/14324-archeologia-da-sant%E2%80%99antioco-a-cleveland-e-ritorno-il-bronzetto-dell%E2%80%99arciere-ritrovato,-by-roberto-lai,-francesca-pitzanti-intervista-by-roberto-lai.html.

31. In addition to the Nuragic archer, thirteen other looted antiquities were returned to Italy, including precious Apulian and Etruscan pottery.

32. Pitzanti, "Archeologia."

33. ICOM Red Lists are available at International Council of Museums (ICOM), "Red List of Cultural Objects at Risk: Yemen," https://icom.museum/wp-content/uploads/2018/05/RL_YEMEN_EN_Pages.pdf, accessed September 25, 2022; see also ICOM, "Red Lists Database," https://icom.museum/en/resources/red-lists/, accessed January 3, 2022.

Contributors

PAOLO CARTA

Paolo Carta is a professor at the University of Trento (Law), where he teaches History of Political Thought and Political Theory. He also serves as dean of the Faculty of Law. He has taught and lectured at the École Normale Supérieure, Columbia University, University of Oxford, Paris Sorbonne, and many other universities and academies. His books include *Leadership* (2022); *Lottare per il diritto* (2020); *Sardinia* (2016); *Francesco Guicciardini tra diritto e politica* (2008); *Ordine giuridico e ordine politico* (2008); *Machiavelli nel XIX e XX secolo* (2007); *Il poeta e la polis* (2003).

GUIDO CLEMENTE

The late Guido Clemente (1942–2021) was a professor of ancient history in the Universities of Pisa and Florence, and specialized in the history of late antiquity (his book on the Notitia Dignitatum has been recently reissued), the late Roman republic and its politics, and modern scholarship of the ancient world. Scoping a wide range of topics and periods, he is considered one of the most distinguished historians of ancient Italy of his generation. His interest in Sardinian ancient history occupied part of his last decade of scholarly activity, and a posthumous book on the topic is forthcoming.

BARBARA FAEDDA

Barbara Faedda is the executive director of the Italian Academy for Advanced Studies at Columbia University and adjunct professor in Columbia's Department of Italian. Her recent publications include *Rule of Law: Cases, Strategies, and Interpretations*, editor (Ronzani/The Italian Academy, 2021); *Elite. Cultura italiana e statunitense tra Settecento e Novecento* (Ronzani, 2020); *From Da Ponte to the Casa Italiana: A Brief History of Italian Studies at Columbia* (Columbia University Press, 2017); *Present and Future Memory. Holocaust Studies at the Italian Academy* (2008–2016), editor (Italian Academy Publications, 2016); "An Italian Perspective on the U.S.-Italy Relationship," in *Italy in the White House: A Conversation on Historical Perspectives* (David M. Rubenstein National Center for White House History, 2016). In 2016 Dr. Faedda conceived the International Observatory for Cultural Heritage (IOCH). In 2019 she was appointed ambassador, permanent observer for the European Public Law Organization to the United Nations. In 2022 the president of the Italian Republic named her a Commander of the Order of Merit of the Italian Republic.

GIUDITTA GIARDINI

Giuditta Giardini is a lawyer serving as a consultant for the Antiquities Trafficking Unit at the Manhattan District Attorney's Office. She holds an LL.M. degree from Columbia Law School. Before moving to New York, she worked for Unidroit, focusing on the *Unidroit Convention on Stolen or Illegally Exported Cultural Objects* (1995). She writes for the "ArtEconomy24" page of the Italian financial newspaper *Il Sole24Ore*. She is a member of the International Council of Museums and the European Law Institute.

MARCO MAIURO

Marco Maiuro was professor of ancient history at Columbia (now adjunct professor of history) and is currently professor of Roman history at Sapienza University of Rome. His scholarly output ranges from pre-Roman to the late antique periods, specializing in social and economic history of the Mediterranean basin. He worked together with Guido Clemente on the second edition of the latter's book on the Notitia Dignitatum and is now editing Clemente's monograph on the ancient history of Sardinia.

—•—

ROBERTO NARDI

Roberto Nardi received a degree in archaeology from the University of Rome and in conservation at the Istituto Centrale per il Restauro in Rome. In 1982 he founded the Archaeological Conservation Center of Rome, a private company acting under public commission in the field of archaeological conservation. He has directed more than fifty projects and training courses in fifteen countries, including the Arch of Septimus Severus in the Roman Forum, the Capitoline museum and the Crypta Balbi in Rome. He received the Europa Nostra Award 2015 for the conservation of the prehistoric sculptures of Mont'e Prama and, for the same project, the Best in Heritage Award 2016.

—•—

ALFONSO STIGLITZ

A specialist archaeologist, Alfonso Stiglitz served as director of the Civic Museum of the Municipality of San Vero Milis (Sardinia), scientific co-director of the excavations conducted by the Municipality of San Vero Milis and Brown University at the site of S'Urachi, and co-scientific director of the excavations by the University of Cagliari in the area of the temple of Astarte in Cagliari (Sardinia). He is the author of one monograph and the editor of three other monographs and approximately one hundred scientific essays. He studies the encounters between cultures in Sardinia in the 1st millennium BCE, and the relation of urban space to rural space. He also conducts research on the influences of racism and nationalism on archaeology.

—•—

EMERENZIANA USAI

Emerenziana Usai graduated from the University of Cagliari in 1975 after studying with Giovanni Lilliu, a leading scholar of Mediterranean prehistory and protohistory. In 1979 she was hired in the Ministry of

Cultural Heritage at the Cagliari Archaeological Superintendency, where she pursued a career as an executive officer of archaeology. She directed numerous archaeological excavations and published more than one hundred studies. In 1979 she participated in the excavations of Mont'e Prama—Cabras, and in 2014 she became co-director of that project on behalf of the Superintendency; she is the author of numerous publications on the findings there. In 2015 she participated in the Study Day on Mont'e Prama hosted in Rome by the Accademia dei Lincei.

PETER VAN DOMMELEN

Peter van Dommelen is an archaeologist studying cultural interactions, indigeneity, and colonialism in the rural West Mediterranean, especially in the Phoenician-Punic world. His research concerns migration, rural landscapes and households, and ancient agriculture, which structure long-term fieldwork and ceramic studies on the island of Sardinia. He serves as director of the Joukowsky Institute of Archaeology and the Ancient World at Brown University and as co-editor of the *Journal of Mediterranean Archaeology*. Publications include *Rural Landscapes of the Punic World* (2008, co-edited with Carlos Gómez Bellard) and *The Cambridge Prehistory of the Bronze and Iron Age Mediterranean* (2014, co-edited with Bernard Knapp).

RAIMONDO ZUCCA

Raimondo Zucca has been a professor of history and archaeology of the ancient Mediterranean at the University of Sassari since 2002. From 1998 to 2002 he was an associate professor there. He has been an archaeological inspector at the Archaeological Superintendency of Cagliari and Oristano (1980–1990) and researcher of Greek and Roman epigraphy at the University of Rome Tor Vergata. He has led archaeological missions in Sardinia (Tharros, Othoca, Neapolis, Forum Traiani, Mont'e Prama), Morocco (Lixus), Tunisia (Neapolis—Nabeul), and Cyprus (Pila Kokkynokremos). He is director of the Antiquarium Arborense (Oristano) and the Othoca Museum (Santa Giusta).